Scottish Railways Then & Now

Scottish Railways Then & Now

Gavin Morrison

Ian Allan
PUBLISHING

Half title page:

Nairn

Then: 1913
The line was opened from Inverness to Nairn on 5 November 1855 by the Inverness & Nairn Railway and thence towards Forres on 22 December 1857. The station is located 15 miles east of Inverness. This busy scene, taken just prior to the outbreak of World War 1, shows the view looking west, towards Inverness. The signalbox at the end of the platform can just be seen. *Ian Allan Library*

Now: 26 May 1998
This station has altered little over the years. Here Class 158 No 158745 is pictured arriving on the 08.06 service from Inverness to Aberdeen at 08.20. The well-maintained station building is shown, together with the little-used goods yard. Today the station has become unique, in that it is served by two signalboxes, located at either end of the very long eastbound platform, which were, on the day of my visit, operated by a single signalwoman who used a bicycle to cycle between the two boxes. The westbound platform is only about half the length of the eastbound. It is reported that Railtrack has plans to replace the signalling at Nairn with colour lights controlled from Forres in the very near future. *Author*

Title page:

Aberdeen (Union Street Bridge)

Then: 7 May 1957
This impressive view is taken from Union Street looking north. A local Class B1 4-6-0, No 61308, threads through the lines towards the Joint station at the head of the 12.19pm service from Elgin. The station was opened on 4 November 1867 by the Aberdeen Station Joint Committee. Services from the north were almost exclusively GNoSR, whilst from the south came trains from the CR and the NBR as well as the GNoSR (from Ballater). *R. K. Evans*

Now: 27 May 1998
It is a sad reflection of the times, but the once impressive railway network at this point has been reduced to a two-track section and a modern dual carriageway has been constructed alongside on the redundant railway infrastructure. The skyline is still similar, although there are now some high-rise flats which hardly blend in with the other buildings. *Author*

Contents

First published 1999

ISBN 0 7110 2684 X

All rights reserved. No part of this book may be reproduced or transmitted in any form or by any means, electronic or mechanical, including photocopying, recording or by any information storage and retrieval system, without permission from the Publisher in writing.

© Ian Allan Publishing Ltd 1999

Published by Ian Allan Publishing

an imprint of Ian Allan Publishing Ltd, Terminal House, Shepperton, Surrey TW17 8AS; and printed by Ian Allan Printing Ltd, Riverdene Business Park, Hersham, Surrey KT12 4RG.

Code: 9910/A2

Introduction

This Scottish volume is the latest in the Ian Allan Publishing Ltd 'Then & Now' series and is the third one in which I have been involved. It was back in October 1994 that I started work on the London Midland volume and, with the Eastern and North Eastern book in between, I have been working on these books for the last four and a half years.

The format is roughly the same as the earlier volumes and once again most of the 'Then' shots have come from my own collection or the Ian Allan Library. You will notice that in some of the 'Now' pictures I have not stood in exactly the same position; this was for a variety of reasons, but usually because, by standing in a slightly different position, it has allowed me to show the changes to better advantage. I have also quite often used a wide-angle lens to increase the coverage of an individual location.

Unlike the two other volumes, when many of the locations were covered by day trips from home, with this volume it has been necessary to set off for several days at a time and it took 24 days of concentrated photography to cover everything you see in these pages. Unfortunately, 1998 must have been one of the wettest summers in Scotland for many years, which made the trips far less enjoyable than one might have hoped; in fact, out of the 24 days, I think we had only three when the sun appeared and on one day, around Paisley (near Glasgow), the roads became so flooded that we had to abandon photography at about 15.00. It is interesting to note that, in spite of the 2,500-mile trip to Wick, Thurso and surrounding areas, the total mileage for this project has only been 5,826, which is about 1,000 less than each of the other two volumes. During the last four years I have covered over 20,000 miles on these books and there are very few parts of the country, other than the south and west, which I have not visited.

I particularly wanted to produce the Scottish album as I have spent so much time travelling about the country since I was a small child, as my father came from Glasgow and most of my relations live in the Glasgow and Edinburgh areas. In addition, I also had two years studying in Glasgow; however, I spent most of my time visiting the Glasgow engine sheds on my bicycle rather than devoting time to my work — with predictable results.

The first trip started at the end of April to Dumfries and we headed towards Stranraer via the 'Port Road'. What a magnificent railway this used to be; fortunately I did see it in action, but travelling in 1998 parallel to it made me realise what vast areas of the country are now without any railways. It was a similar situation in the Border Counties and in the far northeast. It also makes one appreciate the relatively empty roads; on our journey from Stranraer to Girvan via Barrhill we passed one car in 20 miles!

Once again, the local people were of great assistance, except on the occasion when I was approached by an angry farmer who thought I was a sheep rustler and a couple in the Borders who delayed me a considerable time as they couldn't understand why I wanted to take a picture of their very fine garden.

I hope I have managed to produce a reasonable balance of pictures between the various railway companies, although pictures of the Caledonian line just south of Glasgow were not as plentiful as I had expected.

Possibly the most dramatic change of any location featured in the book is of the old Glasgow St Enoch station, which has completely vanished to be replaced by a vast shopping centre. Fortunately, most of the fine main line stations still exist and appear to be well kept; examples that spring to mind are Edinburgh Waverley, Perth, Inverness and, my personal favourite, Glasgow Central. Others, however, such as Edinburgh Princes Street and Glasgow Buchanan Street, as well as St Enoch, are but memories.

Many old stations have become private dwellings and fortunately those stations that are now unmanned on the West Highland and Far North lines do not seem to have suffered from vandalism. Certain closed lines have been converted into cycleways or footpaths; these include the Speyside line and the Buchan route north of Aberdeen. However, I saw very few people making use of the facilities.

Scotland has been very much diesel and electric multiple-unit country for quite a few years and there is now very little freight north of a line between Glasgow and Edinburgh, so the 'Now' photographs produced very few locomotive-hauled trains. The ScotRail services that still exist seem to run extremely well with the

Biggar

Then: 29 March 1964
An RCTS special visited the station at Biggar, located on the ex-CR route from Symington to Peebles, in early 1964, some 14 years after the line had lost its regular passenger services (on 14 August 1950). The section of line from Symington to Broughton opened on 5 November 1860; it was extended eastwards to Peebles on 1 February 1864. *Author*

Now: 20 October 1998
The section between Symington and Broughton was to close completely on 4 April 1966. Today, the station and signalbox still stand and seem to be in reasonable condition. The land is now owned by a company called James Cuthbertson Engineers. *Author*

Class 158 and 156 units, whilst the Strathclyde area sees an excellent service with EMUs in and around Glasgow. Unfortunately, the Edinburgh district does not seem to be blessed with such a system; most of the suburban lines were abandoned in the Beeching era and redeveloped, resulting in dense road traffic problems.

I must again express my sincere thanks to my trusty navigator, Keith Marshall, who worked wonders around the southern Glasgow suburbs when every map we had seemed to be totally out of date, and spent hours sitting in the car keeping dry while I got soaked in the rain. To Peter Waller, again my thanks for adding to and checking some of the information regarding dates of opening and closure and, finally, as with the earlier volumes, to Brian Morrison for some of the 'Then' pictures.

I hope that you, the reader, enjoy seeing the changes at some of the more remote parts of the country which you are unlikely to visit. Scotland suffered badly with the rationalisation of the railways, but the

system seems to have stabilised and what is left appears to be running well, even if the variety of stock and motive power is very limited.

I always like to finish on a positive note. We have heard that proposals are being put forward to reopen the Waverley route for timber traffic from the south to around Riccarton and possibly at the north end for suburban trains. With the recent reintroduction of freight trains in the Far North and West Highlands, these developments suggest that the railways in Scotland will continue to take on an expanding role in the transport of the country.

Gavin Morrison
Mirfield
February 1999

Caledonian Railway

With its blue locomotives and crimson and white coaching stock, the Caledonian was perhaps the most prestigious of the Scottish main line railway companies, incorporating as it did the Royal Arms of Scotland into it crest. Although exceeded in size by the North British, the CR was undoubtedly the more glamorous of the two companies. At its peak, the CR could lay claim to some 1,100 miles of track and 927 locomotives, carrying some 34 million passengers per annum and 23 million tons of mineral traffic. The company's network stretched as far south as Carlisle, representing the Scottish partner in the West Coast main line expresses, as far northeast as Aberdeen, as far northwest as Oban and Ballachulish and east into the heart of North British territory in the Edinburgh area.

The origins of the CR date back to 1845 when an Act was obtained for the construction of a line from Carlisle to Glasgow. Of the two routes available, via Annandale or via Clydesdale, the former — which was the more difficult and included the ascent to Beattock Summit — was selected. The line was engineered by Joseph Locke, engineer of the Grand Junction, and opened from Carlisle to Beattock on 10 September 1847 and thence to Glasgow and Edinburgh on 15 February 1848.

Much of the CR's dominance in the central belt of Scotland came through its mergers with other railway companies. Of these, the two most important in opening up the route to Aberdeen were the Scottish Central and the Scottish North Eastern. The Scottish Central was authorised to construct a 46-mile line from Perth to Castlecary. Incorporated on 31 July 1845, the line was to open throughout on 22 May 1848. It passed to CR ownership by an Act of Parliament dated 5 July 1865. The Scottish North Eastern was itself the result of an amalgamation on 29 July 1856 between the Aberdeen Railway — incorporated on 31 July 1845 to construct a line between Guthrie, on the Arbroath & Forfar Railway with branches to Brechin and Montrose and opened in stages between 1 February 1848 and 2 August 1853 — and the Scottish Midland Junction Railway — which was incorporated on 31 July 1845 to construct a line between Perth and the Aberdeen Railway (opened to passenger services on 4 August 1848) along with various branches (to Blairgowrie and Kirriemuir, for example). The SNER passed to CR control under an Act of 10 August 1866.

Apart from these pivotal lines, the CR was also to gain access to the Highlands through the operation of the Callander & Oban Railway. This line was nominally independent up to the Grouping in 1923, but was operated throughout its life by the CR. Although incorporated on 5 July 1865, it was not until 1 July 1880 that the complete line was opened throughout. The extension from Connel Ferry to Ballachulish was authorised on 7 August 1896 and opened on 24 August 1903.

At the Grouping, the CR, along with the Highland and Glasgow & South Western railways, formed part of the new London, Midland & Scottish Railway. With the NBR merged into the LNER, the traditional rivalry between the two companies was to continue for a further quarter century. The period of the Grouping brought many changes to the CR. As elsewhere, the interwar years brought a number of line closures. Already, by the time that the LMSR was formed, the CR had withdrawn passenger services from a number of lines; these included the horse-tramway, which linked Inchture station with the village of Inchture and which is believed to has ceased operating on 31 December 1916, and the line from Abbey Holme to Brayton (which closed on 20 May 1921). Closures under the auspices of the LMS included Annan-Kirtlebridge (on 27 April 1931), Aidrie-Newhouse (on 1 December 1930), Airdrie-Whifflet (on 3 May 1943), Methven-Methven Junction (on 27 September 1937), Bankfoot-Strathord (13 April 1931), East Kilbride-Blantyre (1 October 1945), Greenhill-Bonnybridge (28 July 1930), Stonehouse-Dalserf (7 January 1935), Brocketsbrae-Hamilton (11 September 1939) and Morningside-Holytown (1 December 1930).

At Nationalisation, traditional rivalries were in theory to have ceased with the merger of the lines of all five of the pre-Grouping companies into the Scottish Region of British Railways. The result of Nationalisation was that gradually many of the duplicate lines were to be rationalised. The elimination of these routes, along with the closure of many of the lines viewed as unremunerative both before and after the Beeching Report, has seen the closure of much of the erstwhile CR network. Amongst the most significant closures have been the complete closure of the erstwhile Callandar & Oban line (with the exception of the section from Crianlarich to Oban which is now served from the ex-NBR West Highland line), the former main line from Stanley Junction to Kinnaber Junction as well as all the ex-CR lines in Angus, all the Edinburgh suburban routes, Edinburgh Princes Street station itself (with services now diverted into Waverley), the ex-CR routes in the Border Counties and much of the intensive network that once served the region between Edinburgh and Glasgow.

Today, the surviving lines that were once owned by the CR form an essential part of the Scottish railway network. The original main line from Edinburgh and Glasgow to Carlisle continues to provide an essential part of the West Coast main line; the line between Edinburgh and Glasgow via Shotts provides an alternative link between Scotland's principal cities; the remaining section of the Callandar & Oban, from Crianlarich to Oban, still offers this part of the Highlands railway access; the erstwhile Scottish Central/Scottish North Eastern main line from Motherwell via Stirling and Perth to Stanley Junction, is the primary route for railway traffic to and from the Highland main line; finally, many of the ex-CR branches in the Glasgow area — such as those to Wemyss Bay and East Kilbride — form an integral part of the electrified network serving the city.

Whilst much of the glamour may have departed from the Caledonian Railway's lines over the past 75 years, much, however, remains in terms of buildings and infrastructure to remind contemporary enthusiasts of the complex network once operated by Scotland's second largest railway company.

Kirkpatrick Fleming

Then: 4 June 1960
This was the first station in Scotland on the West Coast main line. On this occasion, the only unnamed 'Britannia', No 70047, heads the up morning Glasgow-Birmingham service through the station. The section of the Caledonian Railway north from Carlisle to Garriongill opened on 15 February 1848. *Author*

Now: 20 October 1998
The station closed on 13 June 1960, with freight facilities being withdrawn on 6 April 1964. Here Class 86/2 No 86225 *Hardwicke* rushes past the site of the station running about 15min late with the 10.00 service from Edinburgh to Brighton. The station and signalbox have vanished, but the footbridge remains and the yard is now owned by R. Nichol & Co. *Author*

Beattock shed

Then: 20 May 1961
Shed accommodation here seems to date back as far as the late 1840s although the shed was enlarged in various stages up to around 1869. This view was taken at a time when banking duties were in the hands of the Fairburn 2-6-4Ts. Ex-CR 0-4-4T No 55234 was probably the Moffat branch locomotive. Inside the shed on this occasion was Fowler 2-6-4T No 42301. The Fairburn tanks had taken over from the famous 'Wemyss Bay' 4-6-2Ts; all of the latter had spent some time on the bank after leaving Polmadie shed, lasting here until 1947. The shed had various codes: 12F in the 1935 numbering, followed by 68D in 1949 and finally 66F. Banking duties finally ended in 1970, by which time Class 20 diesels were used. *Author*

Now: 29 July 1998
The shed closed in May 1967 when BR standard Class 4MT 2-6-0s were the regular locomotives on the banking duties. The sidings were hardly used for years after the shed was demolished but recently it appears that the loading of timber has started, as seen in this 'Now' photograph. *Author*

Moffat

Then: August 1952
Moffat was situated at the end of a two-mile branch which ran northeast from the West Coast main line at Beattock. The pleasant town served by the branch is located in the Lowther Hills and services over the branch commenced on 2 April 1883. Here ex-CR McIntosh Class 439 0-4-4T No 55221 is pictured at the branch terminus having just arrived from Beattock.
Ian Allan Library (K1627)

Beattock North End

Then: 16 July 1967
On a dismal day, privately owned Gresley Class A4 No 60019 *Bittern* departs from Beattock station with an RCTS special from Leeds to Glasgow. A Class 20 is on a short freight in the background and some 'dead' steam locomotives can be seen dumped at the side of the shed. Beattock station opened, with the rest of the CR main line from Carlisle to Edinburgh and Glasgow, on 15 February 1848. *Author*

Now: 29 July 1998
The station at Beattock closed on 3 January 1972 and has now been demolished along with the goods shed. Here Transrail-liveried Class 56 No 56066 shunts some timber wagons into the yard. Electrification of the West Coast main line through Beattock was inaugurated on 6 May 1974. Apart from electrification and the demolition of the original station, there has also been a reduction in the number of sidings here. *Author*

Now: 29 July 1998
Passenger services over the Moffat branch were withdrawn on 6 December 1954 with freight being withdrawn on 6 April 1964. Part of the station site, as shown here, has been converted into a very attractive park, which is extremely well maintained. *Author*

Beattock Summit

Then: 14 July 1962
Stanier Pacific No 46200 *Princess Royal*, pictured in red livery, is working out its last days at the head of a Euston-Perth express on Bastille Day in 1962 as it passes the summit at Beattock on its northbound journey. Beattock Summit is 1,015ft above sea level and, like the rest of the CR main line between Carlisle and Glasgow, opened on 15 February 1848. Note the snow fences and the loops. *Author*

Now: 29 July 1998
I have taken this picture from a higher viewpoint because it was not easy to get to the trackside as the ground was virtually waterlogged; I also wanted to show the vast amount of tree planting that has taken place over the past 36 years as well as to indicate the presence of the M74 on the east side of the track. The road will stay to the east of the line until it crosses over the railway just south of Beattock, whereas the old A74 was on the west side from Harthorpe viaduct to a point just north of the summit. Clearly visible is the summit sign confirming that the point is 1,015ft above sea level. *Author*

Lamington

Then: July 1965
This pleasant station was situated on the West Coast main line in the Clyde Valley just to the south of Symington. The line through the station opened on 15 April 1848. An unidentified English Electric Type 1 (later Class 20) heads south with a permanent way train. *W. J. V. Anderson*

Now: 29 July 1998
Passenger services at Lamington ceased on 4 January 1965, with freight facilities having been withdrawn the previous year. Today, all traces of the station have vanished except for the approach road to the station itself. *Author*

Carstairs station (north)

Then: 30 June 1963
An RCTS special from Leeds prepares to leave the north end of this junction station, headed by the preserved ex-Highland Railway 'Jones Goods' No 103 piloting ex-CR Class 812 No 57581. The train was heading for the Glasgow & South Western main line at Auchinleck via Muirkirk. The special had been hauled by Gresley Class A4 No 60023 *Golden Eagle* from Leeds to Carlisle and 'Princess Coronation' No 46255 *City of Hereford* from Carlisle to Carstairs, with both locomotives giving lively performances. The station at Carstairs opened on 15 February 1848 and became a major intersection on the West Coast main line north of Carlisle, being the point where the Edinburgh sections of expresses were attached or detached. There was also a locomotive shed; this was situated alongside the station on the up side. *Author*

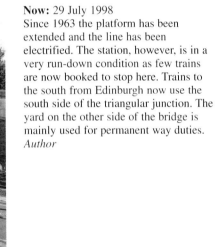

Now: 29 July 1998
Since 1963 the platform has been extended and the line has been electrified. The station, however, is in a very run-down condition as few trains are now booked to stop here. Trains to the south from Edinburgh now use the south side of the triangular junction. The yard on the other side of the bridge is mainly used for permanent way duties. *Author*

Motherwell

Then: 29 September 1962
One of the 'Blue Train' EMUs enters the station on a Hamilton-Glasgow Central service. The first station at Motherwell opened on 20 March 1841 but was replaced by the second station, that illustrated here, on 31 July 1885. The main line platforms are to the left of the picture (out of view). *S. Rickard*

Lanark

Then: 16 October 1965
The station is situated on a short spur from the ex-CR line which used to link the CR main line with the GSWR main line at Auchinleck via Muirkirk. The line from Cleghorn, where there was a triangular junction, to Lanark opened as a single-track branch under the auspices of the Lanark Railway to freight on 5 January 1855. The branch passed to the CR in 1860; it was doubled and opened for passenger traffic, along with the line west to Douglas, on 1 April 1864. Here the preserved ex-GNoSR Class D40 4-4-0 No 49 *Gordon Highlander* was working a special in the area. It is pictured about to depart from Lanark before heading to Carstairs and Edinburgh. *Author*

Now: 29 July 1998
The line has now been singled with two platforms at the terminus. The line was electrified from 1974 and here Class 314 No 314212 has just arrived from Glasgow Central. The skyline has altered with the demolition of the church, but the house on the extreme right of the 'Then' picture can still be seen. *Author*

Now: 20 October 1998
With the rain bouncing off the platform, the scene has changed considerably over the past 36 years. The trees have obscured the buildings on the right and the station has been considerably modernised. What I believe was a bay platform visible on the left of the 'Then' picture has been filled in. One thing, however, is unchanged: 36 years on, the Class 303 EMUs are still passing through the station. *Author*

Motherwell Lesmahagow Junction

Then: 21 March 1963
Humble duties for the only BR-built 'Princess Coronation',
No 46257 *City of Salford*, sees the locomotive taking the Perth line at
the head of a van train. By this date, the locomotive was entering the
autumn of its career; it was to be withdrawn in September 1964.
Lesmahagow Junction is the point where the line towards Stirling
and Perth headed north from the CR main line into Glasgow. The
link from Motherwell, to the Scottish Central line at Castlecary
(north of Cumbernauld) opened on 7 August 1848. *D. C. Smith*

Now: 22 October 1998
This used to be a good location to photograph trains heading towards
Stirling and Perth, but as can be seen electrification has now ruined
it. On this occasion, a couple of Strathclyde Class 303 units, with
No 303006 leading, are seen passing through the junction. *Author*

Coatbridge Central

Then: July 1955
An ex-works Class 5 No 44725 of Carlisle Kingmoor shed is at the head of a Perth-Euston express. It is shown approaching the station. The station opened in March 1843 and was renamed 'Coatbridge Central' on 8 June 1953. *Ian Allan Library*

Now: 22 October 1998
The sidings on the down side have gone and a new housing development has appeared in the background. The bridges in the background of the 'Then' photograph are now no more. Electrification is now in place — inaugurated on 11 August 1981 — and the line is today busy with local passenger and freight services. Strathclyde-liveried Class 101 unit No 101690 is just leaving for Cumbernauld as Class 156 Sprinter No 156494, in the new Strathclyde livery, approaches from the north. *Author*

Polmadie shed

Then: 20 May 1953
The original shed was constructed of timber around 1875, but this material did not prove long-lasting and the old 14-road construction was rebuilt in 1923. The new building was a vast structure and on a Sunday, in the 1940s or 1950s, there were usually around 160 locomotives present. This made Polmadie the largest shed in Scotland and one of the largest on the railway network. Eastfield, on the opposite side of Glasgow, could provide around 140 during the same period. The variety of motive power varied from ex-CR 0-6-0Ts to 'Princess Coronation' Pacifics. This view at the north end shows local 'Clan' No 72004 *Clan MacDonald* receiving attention with 'Jubilee' No 45599 *Bechuanaland* alongside. *Author*

Now: 22 October 1998
The old main shed has been completely demolished. The building, which has survived from the steam era, is the old repair shed. This is still in use and is seen in the left background of this view. Stabled in the sidings is Class 86/2 No 86227 *Sir Henry Johnson.* Also visible is local Class 08 No 08887 in a one-off livery. *Author*

Balnornock/St Rollox shed

Then: 12 April 1959
During the reorganisation and electrification of Glasgow (Central) station in this period, West Coast main line services were diverted to Glasgow (Buchanan Street), which resulted in 'Princess Royal' and 'Princess Coronation' Pacifics appearing at St Rollox shed. This shed, coded '65B', was also known as Balnornock. Polmadie-allocated 'Princess Royal' No 46201 *Princess Elizabeth* descends the 1 in 79 gradient from Robroyston to Buchanan Street with the empty stock which would later form the service to Birmingham (New Street). This view was taken from the road bridge carrying Broomfield Road and shows a number of locomotives on shed at St Rollox; these include Kingmoor-allocated 'Clan' No 72005 *Clan Macgregor*, Crewe North 'Princess Coronation' No 46228 *Duchess of Rutland* and Ivatt 2-6-0 No 43140. The shed provided motive power for the line to Oban as well as for other services over ex-CR metals to the north. Towards the end of steam, Gresley 'A4' No 60031 *Golden Plover* was allocated to the shed, but St Rollox is probably best remembered for the four named Class 5s which spent many years working from it. About 70 locomotives represented a typical allocation during the 1950s. *Author*

Polmadie

Then: August 1965
This view, taken looking north, was photographed from the road bridge that crossed the West Coast main line at the south end of Polmadie shed (66A). Rebuilt 'Royal Scot' No 46140, without nameplates but formerly named *The King's Royal Rifle Corps*, is on an empty stock movement. The date of the photograph is some three months before the locomotive's withdrawal. In the background can be seen a BR Standard Class 4MT; this appears to be No 80109. *D. Cameron*

Now: 22 October 1998
As usual, the bushes have grown up in the background and the skyline has altered. The track layout has also been altered, no doubt when the line was electrified. Strathclyde-liveried Class 101 No 101694 is shown heading for Glasgow Central. *Author*

Now: 22 October 1998
Everything has changed here and it is hard to believe that the shed ever existed. The track alignment has been altered to the north in order to cross over a new dual carriageway. New houses have been built on the skyline as well as on the site of the shed itself. The lines to the right have also gone; these used to lead into St Rollox Works. Here Class 47/7 No 47732 *Restormel* passes light engine heading towards Cowlairs. *Author*

Glasgow Central (view south)

Then: April 1955
The Caledonian Railway opened its first station for central Glasgow — Bridge Street — on the south side of the River Clyde on 12 August 1840. It was extended on 12 July 1879 and eventually closed on 1 March 1905. Permission to build a bridge over the river was given in 1873 and Central station first opened on 1 August 1879. A second bridge across the river was built between 1901 and 1906 due to the vast increase in traffic, at which time Central station itself was also enlarged. The down 'Royal Scot' is shown approaching the station in the evening sun headed by an immaculate Polmadie-allocated 'Princess Coronation' No 46231 *Duchess of Atholl*. The locomotive spent 22 years of its 24-year career allocated to the Glasgow shed. *Author*

Now: 28 October 1998
The bridge through which the 'Royal Scot' passed in the 'Then' photograph became surplus to requirements during the extensive track and signalling reorganisation in 1961 and was eventually dismantled. The change here, as a result, has been dramatic. The bridge has gone and high-rise flats now dominate the skyline. Strathclyde Class 303 No 303080 makes a cautious exit from the station through the complex trackwork with a service for Neilston. *Author*

Glasgow Central (view north)

Then: 21 July 1959
An immaculate red-liveried 'Princess Coronation', No 46240 *City of Coventry*, which was allocated to Camden shed, makes a spirited departure from Glasgow at the start of its 401-mile journey to London Euston. It is departing from Platform 3; the usual departure platform for the up 'Royal Scot' was No 2. *Author*

Now: 28 October 1998
This was the scene at the end of Platform 2 on a wet October day in 1998. Apart from the arrival of the electrification masts, most of the background structures are still largely the same as they were 40 years ago. The very busy scene shows Class 86/2 No 86222 *Clothes Show Live* preparing to depart, Class 156 Sprinter No 156512 arriving, GNER DVT No 82207 heading a King's Cross-bound train and Virgin-liveried DVT No 82149 at the head of an up Euston express. *Author*

Partick Central

Then: 5 August 1957
Ex-CR McIntosh Class 812 0-6-0 No 57607 pulls away from the station at the head of a Dalmuir-Rutherglen train. In the background are the Spillers' Scotstoun Mills. The train is seen crossing the River Kelvin before entering Stobcross Tunnel. The station was renamed 'Kelvin Hall' on 15 June 1959, prior to the opening of the Scottish Industries Exhibition.
G. H. Robin

Now: 21 October 1998
Passenger services over the line through Partick Central ceased on 5 October 1964 at which time the line east from Partick Central Goods to Tollcross closed completely. The River Kelvin was on this occasion a raging torrent due to the amount of rain. The bridge is still in place although the track is long since gone. Part of the old Scotstoun Mill still stands. It was not possible to stand in exactly the same place as the West Scotland Engineering Co has built part of its plant on the site. *Author*

Edinburgh (Princes Street)

Then: July 1958
This immaculate locally-based Stanier Class 5 No 45166 looks as if it has been on Royal train duties, judging by the polished buffers. Allocated to Dalry Road shed at the time, it stands inside a very deserted Princes Street station. This fine station, which never attracted the attention that Waverley did, was first opened on 2 May 1870. The original — 'temporary'! — station was destroyed by fire on 16 June 1890 and the replacement station, as illustrated here, was opened in stages during 1894. There were fine photographs to be obtained here, as well as at Waverley, and the Polmadie Pacifics were often to be spotted here, between their Anglo-Scottish main line duties.
Ian Allan Library (K3803)

Cobbinshaw

Then: 25 May 1963
This remote station is about a third of the way between Carstairs and Edinburgh. The first station here opened on 15 February 1848 along with the route from Carstairs to Edinburgh, but it was replaced by this station on 4 October 1875. Here Stanier Class 5 No 44976 departs with the 1.20pm Edinburgh (Princes Street)-Lanark service. *W. A. C. Smith*

Now: 20 October 1998
Cobbinshaw station was closed on 18 April 1966 and by 1998 all traces of the station have disappeared. The line is now electrified and sees regular services operated by GNER from Glasgow Central to London King's Cross via Edinburgh Waverley. *Author*

Now: 7 February 1999
The Caledonian Hotel, which provided the station's facade on to Princes Street itself, is still very much in business, but behind the facade all has changed. Princes Street closed on 6 September 1965 and the site of the platforms has now been completely redeveloped with a road and modern offices. *Author*

Craigleith

Then: Undated (early 1950s) Caledonian McIntosh '812' class 0-6-0 No 57559, which was a local Dalry Road-allocated locomotive, passes the junction at Craigleith heading the 1.43pm from Leith North to Edinburgh (Princes Street). The line on the left went to Davidson's Main and Barnton. The Leith North branch saw its first passenger services on 1 August 1879 and the Davidson's Main line opened on 1 March 1894. *G. M. Staddon/ Neville Stead Collection*

Now: 29 July 1998 It is hard to believe that this is the same location as the trees have completely obliterated the view. The picture was taken from the pavement of the busy A90 to the Forth Bridge from Edinburgh centre. The trackbed is now a cycleway/footpath, as can just be seen through the leaves. The Davidson's Main line lost its passenger services on 7 May 1951 and was to close completely on 1 June 1960. Passenger services ceased between Edinburgh and Leith North on 30 April 1962 and the line subsequently closed completely. *Author*

Grangemouth (Fouldubs Junction)

Then: 20 June 1963 An ex-North British Class J37 0-6-0 No 64621 trundles past Fouldubs Junction heading towards Grangemouth. In the background — looking to the south — the motive power shed can be seen. It is believed that it was completed in 1875; it eventually became a sub-depot of Eastfield in the diesel era. The shed carried several different codes: in 1935 it was 28C under Motherwell, then 31D under St Rollox and finally 65F. The first railway to Grangemouth was opened in 1860 under the auspices of the Forth & Clyde Canal; was eventually to pass to the CR in 1867 although was physically separated from the rest of the CR network and could only be accessed through running powers over the NBR. The line to the west from Fouldubs Junction provided an alternative link to the ex-NBR main line; it was completed in 1908 as a result of booming traffic through the port at Grangemouth. *S. Rickard*

Leith North

Then: 11 February 1961
This was the terminus of the branch from Edinburgh (Princes Street). The line opened on 1 August 1879 with the station being renamed 'Leith North' on 1 August 1903. By the date of the photograph, freight to Leith North had ceased — some nine years earlier — although passenger services remained operational. Fairburn 2-6-4T No 42271 is seen arriving with a service; the steam locomotive had replaced the regular DMU as a result of a rugby match being played at Murrayfield. *W. S. Sellar*

Now: 29 July 1998
My thanks are due to the management of Newhaven Purvis Marquees for allowing me to take this picture in their yard. Just to the left of the picture one could still find the platform edge. The picture was taken from a slightly lower viewpoint than the 'Then' photograph. *Author*

Now: 25 October 1998
The view has now been blocked in part by the M9 motorway. The tracks into the shed area are still in existence, but the shed and the immediate area are now derelict. The Grangemouth branch lost its passenger services on 29 January 1968. The line remains busy with freight to and from the various freight terminals at Grangemouth. The 1908 route was closed completely west of Orchardhall on 12 August 1968, but remains open from Fouldubs Junction to serve Orchardhall. *Author*

Larbert

Then: May 1955
The station board says 'Larbert for Stenhousemuir and Carron'. This station opened on 1 March 1848. This scene shows one of the locally allocated Midland Compounds, No 40938, calling with a stopping train from Glasgow (Buchanan Street) to Stirling, whilst on the left is ex-CR Class 432 0-4-4T No 55238 ready to leave on a train which was probably heading for Alloa. *Ian Allan Library (K2585)*

Now: 25 October 1998
The station remains in use today but the bay platform and the centre roads have gone and the building in the background has been altered. The station is still busy with services to the north from both Edinburgh and Glasgow. *Author*

Stirling (south)

Then: 1 March 1963
Class B1 4-6-0 No 61102 heads south of Stirling on an up train and passes the steam shed. This structure originally dated back to 1850. Even in the latter days of steam in the area, there were plenty of ex-CR 0-6-0s in the allocation, along with Stanier Class 5s. The shed provided much of the motive power for the Oban line. This picture was taken from the road bridge. *R. T. Hughes*

Wemyss Bay

Then: 8 July 1965
This was the terminus of the Caledonian branch built along the south side of the River Clyde. The line opened on 13 May 1865. The station was built next to the pier and the trains connected with the Clyde steamers to Rothesay. In the years after World War 2, the station was extremely busy at weekends during the summer. Polmadie-allocated Standard Class 5MT No 73075 is pictured departing from the station with a service for Glasgow (Central). *P. Paye*

Now: 28 April 1998
There are now only two platforms in use at the station, but these are sufficient to cater for the basically hourly service to Glasgow. On the day of my visit, the late afternoon trains were being worked by Class 303 EMUs. The line was electrified from 5 September 1967. The station has been extensively renovated in recent years and is a delight to see — well worth a visit. *Author*

Now: 25 October 1998
All signs of the depot have now vanished and nature appears to have taken over. The 11.17 service from Aberdeen to Glasgow (Queen Street) passes the site; the train is formed of Class 158 units Nos 158744 and 158737. *Author*

Stirling (north)

Then: 8 June 1957
This busy scene was taken from the road bridge at the north end of the station. It shows Caprotti Standard Class 5MT No 73146, allocated to Glasgow St Rollox (65B), which has just arrived with a Glasgow (Buchanan Street)-Dundee (West) express, whilst Carlisle Kingmoor-allocated Class 5 No 45334 waits on some empty stock and local Standard Class 4MT No 80125 undertakes some shunting. The line from Castlecary to Perth via Stirling was constructed under the auspices of the Scottish Central Railway and opened from Larbert to Stirling on 1 March 1848 and thence to Perth on 23 May 1848. *Author*

Now: 25 October 1998
Apart from changes to the skyline, this location has altered little over the past 40 years; in fact the station appears to be in better condition than it was in 1957. *Author*

Gleneagles

Then: 11 May 1963
No doubt over the years, many famous golfers and other dignitaries have boarded and alighted from trains at this station, but whilst it is still open, the station is now unstaffed and lacks the air of importance which it once seemed to have. Here Standard Class 5MT No 73007 was the surprise motive power for the one-coach train to Crieff. It was probably standing in for a failed four-wheel railbus, as the latter had taken over normal services by this date. The section of the Scottish Central Railway from Stirling to Perth via Gleneagles opened on 23 May 1848. Gleneagles became a junction with the opening of the branch to Crieff via Muthill on 16 March 1856. *Author*

Dunblane

Then: 13 June 1959
Dunblane, on the section of the Scottish Central Railway which opened between Stirling and Perth on 23 May 1848, was to become the junction for the Callander & Oban line with the opening of the latter route on 1 July 1858. The junction was situated at the north end of the station. This view is from the road bridge at the south end and shows Stirling-allocated Class 5 No 45359 working a train from Callander to Stirling. *Author*

Now: 25 October 1998
Apart from the new footbridge and station lamps, along with alterations to the station buildings, this location has changed little over the last 39 years. The station is, however, no longer a junction; the line to Callander lost its passenger services, and was to close completely, on 1 November 1965. *Author*

Now: 26 October 1998
Apart from the removal of the track and the usual growth of bushes, the station remains basically unchanged. The branch to Crieff lost its passenger services on 6 July 1964 and was to close completely between Gleneagles and Muthill on the following 1 September. *Author*

Crieff

Then: July 1963

This station was situated about halfway along the line from Balquhidder to Perth and was the junction for the line southwards to Gleneagles. The first line at Crieff was that to Gleneagles, which opened on 16 March 1856. Ten years later, on 21 May 1866, the town was linked with Methven Junction. Finally, the line was extended westwards to Comrie, and a new station opened, on 1 July 1893. On this occasion in July 1963 the midday train for Gleneagles was being hauled by Class 5 No 45465; the duty represented an easy task for the locomotive. *M. Pope*

Now: 26 October 1998

It is only recently that the station site has been cleared and a new Somerfield supermarket constructed. All traces of the station have now vanished. Passenger services between Crieff and Methven (Perth) ceased on 1 October 1951 although the line remained open for freight until 11 September 1967. Passenger services over the Gleneagles-Comrie line ceased on 6 July 1964. The line from Crieff to Comrie was to close completely at the same time; the stump of the line to Gleneagles, the section south from Crieff to Muthill, was to close completely on 2 November 1964. *Author*

Comrie

Then: July 1958
Perth-allocated ex-CR Class 72 4-4-0 No 54500 is shown ready to leave with a train for Gleneagles during July 1958. The line westwards from Crieff to Comrie opened on 1 July 1893; it was to be extended further west to St Fillans on 1 October 1901 and thence to Lochearnhead on 1 July 1904. By the date of the 'Then' photograph, Comrie was again the terminus of the route with the line between Comrie and Lochearnhead closing completely on 1 October 1951.
Ian Allan Library (K3810)

Now: 26 October 1998
Comrie retained its passenger services until 6 July 1964 at which time the line west of Crieff was closed completely. The site of the station has now been developed into a pleasant caravan park, with the only indication that the railway ever existed being the old road overbridge which is hidden in the trees in the background. *Author*

St Fillans

Then: Undated (pre-1923)
This station was opened on 1 October
1901 with the extension of the line
westwards from Comrie. It was destined
to remain a terminus until the opening
of the line to Lochearnhead on 1 July
1904. The train is heading towards
Crieff. *Ian Allan Library*

Now: 25 October 1998
Passenger services through St Fillans
ceased when the line between Comrie
and Lochearnhead closed completely on
1 October 1951. It was a great surprise
to find on my visit that the station,
signalbox and platforms were still in
existence and in excellent condition,
having been very well preserved as part
of the caravan site which now occupies
the site. I have included an extra picture
to show the station building. *Author
(both)*

Perth (south)

Then: 13 August 1965
This picture was taken from the road bridge which is situated above the north end of Moncrieff Tunnel. The tunnel emerges at the south end close to Hilton Junction, where the ex-NB line towards Fife joins the Scottish Central Railway route into Perth. Situated about one mile south of the station, in 1965 one was able to obtain from this location a commanding view of the railway. The shed (63A) can be seen in the background, with some Class 5s stored in the siding opposite.

Steam traction in the area was very much in decline by this date, although the main Aberdeen and Dundee services into Glasgow were still steam-hauled. Here St Rollox (65B)-allocated Caprotti Standard Class 5MT No 73151 is about to enter the tunnel at the head of the morning Dundee (West)-Glasgow (Buchanan Street) express. The Scottish Central line from Stirling to Perth opened on 23 May 1848. *Author*

Now: 26 October 1998
The bushes have now grown to such an extent that the houses to the left of the 'Then' picture have disappeared. The footbridge across the line, which used to pass the shed, is still intact and now leads to a shopping centre. The sidings, however, are but a memory. The whole makes for a dramatic change over the past 33 years. The daily GNER service from Inverness to King's Cross is seen heading south on its way towards Edinburgh via Stirling. *Author*

Perth station (south)

Then: July 1955/16 August 1965
I have included two 'Then' pictures for the south end of Perth station, which, by use of a wide-angle lens, can both be compared with one 'Now' picture. The station was opened on 23 May 1848 with the opening of the line from Stirling. The line was extended northwards to Stanley Junction and beyond on 20 August 1848, whilst the line across the River Tay towards Dundee was opened on 1 March 1849. The station was renamed 'Perth General' in 1952. Perth was an important railway centre as the gateway to the Highlands, as well as serving lines towards Dundee, Edinburgh, Glasgow and Crieff. There were originally two locomotive sheds, which eventually merged. Perth was one of the few locations where both ex-LMS and ex-LNER Pacifics could be seen alongside each other. The first picture shows local Class 5 No 45460 piloting another member of the class ready to depart on an Inverness-Glasgow service, with an ex-CR 0-4-4T on station pilot duties. Another Class 5, No 44721, is also ready to leave on an up local service. The second 'Then' shot shows, over on the Dundee side, Carlisle Kingmoor-allocated 'Britannia' No 70003, formerly named *John Bunyan*, ready to leave, without having taken water on an up troop train.
Ian Allan Library (K2665)/Author

Now: 26 October 1998
The south end of the station has altered little over the years, except that the freight yards to the left of the picture are very overgrown. Elsewhere in Perth the railway has been dramatically rationalised, with the site of the old steam shed (63A) now being occupied by a supermarket. Perth is still a busy railway centre, but passenger services are now almost exclusively formed by Class 158 units. There is currently very little freight traffic. *Author*

Dundee (West)

Then: March 1958

Dundee (West) was one of three stations to serve the city and the station illustrated here was the third to serve the line towards Perth, opening in 1889. The line opened from Dundee to Barnhill on 24 May 1847 and thence into Perth on 1 March 1849. Here one of the Caprotti Standard Class 5MT 4-6-0s allocated to St Rollox shed, No 73148, is shown leaving the station with a service to Glasgow (Buchanan Street). On the right an ex-NBR Class C16 4-4-2T is probably on station pilot duties. *W. J. V. Anderson*

Now: 27 October 1998

Passenger services were withdrawn from Dundee (West) on 3 May 1965 and the station, with its superb baronial-style facade, was demolished the following year. Part of the site, closest to the city centre, has already been redeveloped and work was in progress clearing the remainder of the site. It was very difficult to know where the platforms used to be, particularly as the tower with the clock featured in the 'Then' photograph (being part of the station facade) has disappeared. No doubt within the next 12 months the site will have been completely redeveloped. *Author*

Dundee shed

Then: 5 June 1953
The ex-NBR main line can be seen on the right climbing towards the Tay Bridge, with Esplanade station just out of the picture. This station lost its passenger services on 2 October 1939 although the platforms survive. Here Gresley 'V2' No 60922 makes a vigorous departure along the ex-CR line towards Perth with special train of 33 vans loaded with jute — now also a thing of the past as far as Dundee is concerned — heading for Kidderminster. The ex-CR engine shed can be seen in the background, although the coaling stage visible in the distance was situated at the adjacent ex-NBR Tay Bridge shed. In spite of the ex-CR shed's size, it only had an allocation of 28 locomotives in 1933. The shed was frequently used to store locomotives, particularly as Tay Bridge shed, albeit modernised, was an extremely cramped location. *BR*

Now: 27 October 1998
The whole of the ex-CR land has been cleared and by late 1998 was in the process of being redeveloped. The shed was used for a number of years as a DMU depot (latterly coded 'DE' by BR), although this function ceased in the early 1980s. Much of the railway land on the western approaches to Dundee — both ex-CR and ex-NBR — has undergone redevelopment in recent years with the decline of freight traffic to the city. *Author*

Stanley Junction

Then: 1932
This view was taken from the bridge at the south end of the station looking northeast. The lines on the left form the ex-Highland Railway main line north towards Inverness, whilst those on the right are the ex-CR main line towards Forfar and Aberdeen. The station was located seven miles north of Perth on the section of line which opened on 20 August 1848. The HR line from the north was opened between Stanley Junction and Dunkeld on 7 April 1856. *Ian Allan Library*

Luncarty

Then: Pre-1923
This station was situated about 4.5 miles north of Perth. The line from Perth northwards to Stanley Junction and thence to Forfar and Glamis opened on 20 August 1848. This undated photograph shows Highland Railway 'Jones Goods' No 114 heading south with an up freight. These fine locomotives were built by Sharp Stewart in 1894. No 114 became LMS No 17927 in 1923 and when new was based at Inverness. It is running with a shortened chimney and was to remain in service until September 1936.
Ian Allan Library/ Bucknall Collection

Now: 21 May 1998
Passenger services were withdrawn from Luncarty on 18 June 1951 and today, whilst the line is still operational, there is absolutely no evidence that a station once existed. The only reference point is the road overbridge in the background. *Author*

Now: 21 May 1998
Stanley Junction station closed on 11 June 1956, whilst freight facilities lasted until 6 December 1965. Despite being the original main line from Glasgow to Aberdeen, the route via Forfar lost its passenger services on 4 September 1967 and was to close completely east of Stanley Junction on 5 June 1982. Little now remains to remind travellers of the location's former importance: just a single line and signalbox. Just to the south of this location, however, the line becomes double track. The 14.25 service from Inverness to Glasgow (Queen Street) passes the former junction, formed of Class 158 No 158743. *Author*

Blairgowrie

Then: August 1952
This station was situated at the end of a branch which left the Stanley Junction-Forfar main line at Coupar Angus. The branch opened originally on 1 August 1855 and did not quite achieve its centenary, losing its passenger services on 10 January 1955. Just under three years earlier, an ex-CR 0-4-4T is shown ready to depart the station with a train for Dundee. *Ian Allan Library*

Now: 26 October 1998
Freight continued to operate over the Blairgowrie branch until 6 December 1965. The site is now owned by Tayside Council. The site provides space for offices as well as storage of materials for building purposes. My thanks are due to the local officers for allowing me to take this photograph. *Author*

Newtyle

Then: Undated (pre-Grouping)
Newtyle was about one mile south of Alyth Junction (on the Stanley Junction-Forfar line) and was the first station on the line southwards towards Dundee. The Dundee & Newtyle Railway was one of the oldest railways in Scotland, being opened on 16 December 1831. It was constructed originally to the unusual gauge of 4ft 6.5in and was provided with three inclined planes — later replaced by deviations — at Auchterhouse, Lochee and Newtyle itself. The line, still at 4ft 6.5in was extended to both Coupar Angus and Glamis in 1837. The line was subsequently regauged to standard gauge. This undated view shows the second station at Newtyle; this opened on 31 August 1868 when the line at Newtyle was realigned to eliminate the inclined plane. *Ian Allan Library*

Coupar Angus

Then: 31 May 1966
Perth-allocated Class 5 No 44997 is
shown shunting the yard after arriving
with a freight from Perth. The railway
first reached Coupar Angus with an
extension of the Dundee & Newtyle's
line from Newtyle in 1837, but the
location's importance grew with the
arrival of the main line from Perth to
Forfar on 20 August 1848, the new
station replacing the original structure
which had closed the previous year.
C. W. R. Bowman

Now: 26 October 1998
I had some difficulty in locating the
station site, having to ask several local
people. The link between the two
photographs is the wall running across
the picture, but the station area is now
owned by the local council and was
being used as a dump for winter road
salt. All traces of the station have
disappeared. The Stanley Junction-
Forfar line lost its passenger services on
4 September 1967 and the line was to
close completely on 5 June 1982. The
freight service, latterly running thrice a
week, ran for the last time on 17 May
1982, the line's closure being marked by
a special train organised by the Angus
Railway Group. *Author*

Now: 26 October 1998
Passenger services via Newtyle ceased
on 1 October 1955. The line closed
completely south of Newtyle to
Auchterhouse on 5 May 1958 and the
section from Newtyle to Alyth Junction
was to close completely on 7 September
1964. The station building still survives
and appeared to be in use by a local
company. Other railway land, however,
had seen new houses built right up to
the station. *Author*

Monikie

Then: 13 March 1967
Monikie was located about one third of the way along the line from Dundee to Forfar. The line opened on 12 August 1870. Here Class B1 4-6-0 No 61347 was working the local pick-up freight along the branch. The train appears ready to leave in the Forfar direction. By the date of this photograph, passenger services over the route had already ceased — on 10 January 1955 — and the line had already closed completely (as from 8 December 1958) from the section between Kingsmuir and Forfar. *W. J. Webster*

Now: 26 October 1998
The section of line from Broughty Ferry, on the Dundee & Arbroath Joint line, to Kingsmuir, via Monikie, closed completely on 9 October 1967. Today one has to look deep into the undergrowth to find some remains of the old platform; as can be seen, the site has been completely taken over by nature. *Author*

Forfar Junction (east)

Then: 25 July 1955

Forfar used to be an important railway intersection with lines radiating out to Perth, Aberdeen, Brechin and Dundee. This view was taken from a road bridge to the east of the station and shows Perth-allocated Stanier Class 5 No 44999 arriving with an up fish train from Aberdeen. The line towards Dundee can be seen leaving to the right. The first railway to reach Forfar was that from the east — Guthrie on the line towards Aberdeen — which opened on 1 March 1839. The line was extended westwards to Glamis on 20 August 1848. Forfar became a junction with the opening of the Dundee line from Broughty Ferry on 12 August 1870. The final piece in the jigsaw came with the opening of the Brechin line on 7 January 1895. A four-road engine shed served Forfar; on the occasion of my visit for the 'Now' photograph, this structure still stood and was in use for industrial purposes. *K. L. Cook*

Now: 26 October 1998

The road bridge still exists, but it now crosses derelict land, although it appeared that earth had recently been deposited. The main line from Perth to Kinnaber Junction lost its passenger services on 4 September 1967 at which time the line east of Forfar was to close completely. The line towards Dundee had, by the date of the 'Then' photograph already lost its passenger services — on 10 January 1955 — and the line south from Forfar to Kingsmuir was to close completely on 8 December 1958. The line to Brechin had also lost its passenger services by 1955 — on 4 August 1952 — and was to close completely on 4 September 1967 from Forfar to Justinhaugh. The line from Stanley Junction to Forfar remained open for freight until 5 June 1982 when two specials hauled by Class 40 No 40143 marked the line's closure. *Author*

Brechin

Then: 4 April 1966
The railways first reached Brechin on 1 February 1848 with the opening of the line from Dubton via Bridge of Dun. The line from Forfar arrived on 7 January 1895. Brechin was provided with a terminus station, which was at the west side of a triangle formed with the Forfar-Bridge of Dun line. Passenger services over both routes to Brechin ceased on 4 August 1952. The line to Careston (on the route to Forfar) closed completely on 17 March 1958. The Edzell branch closed completely on 7 September 1964. At this date, therefore, Brechin was purely a freight-only destination served from the Bridge of Dun direction. Class J37 No 64620 is seen on this occasion at the head of the 1.40pm pick-up freight from Montrose. *J. M. Boyes*

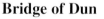

Now: 26 October 1998
Freight traffic over the branch continued until 3 May 1981 when the line from Kinnaber Junction closed completely. Latterly, the main traffic to Brechin was coal and lime from Coxhoe in Durham. Following the line's closure, the section from Brechin to Bridge of Dun was preserved by the new Caledonian Railway. This was the scene at the end of October when services had ceased for the year. The station building has lost its platform awnings, but is otherwise largely intact. *Author*

Bridge of Dun

Then: Undated
The station was situated at the junction where the line to Brechin and Forfar left the Caledonian main line from Kinnaber Junction to Forfar via Guthrie. The lines through Bridge of Dun all opened simultaneously on 1 February 1848. This view, taken looking east from the road bridge, shows the Caledonian main line heading towards Aberdeen. The platform arrangements and junction for the line towards Brechin are also clearly defined. *Ian Allan Library*

Edzell

Then: 19 May 1964
This was the terminus of a short branch that ran due north from the Forfar-Brechin line. The line opened on 1 June 1896 but by the date of this photograph, passenger services had already been withdrawn (on 27 April 1931). These were temporarily reinstated on 4 July 1938 until 26 September 1938, but not thereafter. Freight, however, continued to operate over the line and on this occasion, despite it being an ex-Caledonian Railway branch, services were being worked by ex-NBR Class J37 No 64577. *J. Spencer Gilks*

Now: 26 October 1998
Freight services between Edzell and Brechin finally ceased on 7 September 1964. There was either a bridge or an embankment at the south end of the yard when the 'Then' photograph was taken. This had been removed, no doubt, when the former railway land had been redeveloped for housing. The church tower in the background clearly defines the location. *Author*

Now: 26 October 1998
Following complete closure of the ex-CR main line east from Forfar to Bridge of Dun on 4 September 1967, the line from Kinnaber Junction to Bridge of Dun was retained to provide access to the Brechin branch. Although Brechin had lost its passenger services on 4 August 1952, it remained open for freight until 4 May 1981. Following closure, the line from Bridge of Dun to Brechin was preserved by the new Caledonian Railway. It reopened in 1987 and runs for 3.5 miles through the Angus landscape. A considerable quantity of railway rolling stock was present on this occasion, which occurred after the main running season had ceased. An operational Class 26 No D5314 can be seen at the rear of the centre road and an Ivatt 2-6-0 was in course of restoration. Most services are usually operated by industrial locomotives. *Author*

Cove Bay

Then: 21 June 1964
Although the line from Portlethan to Ferryhill (Aberdeen) opened on 1 April 1850, it was not until 1 October 1912 that this station, situated six miles south of Aberdeen, was opened. By the date of this photograph, passenger services had already been withdrawn (on 11 June 1956) and freight facilities had also succumbed (on 28 October 1963). The dirty Class V2 No 60834 looks rather out of place as it passes on a two-coach local service from Perth to Aberdeen. *J. S. Rindley*

Now: 27 May 1998
All signs of the station have now vanished. Ironically, in the 34 years since the 'Then' photograph was taken, the area has seen a considerable boom in the number of houses, evidence of which is clearly shown in this view. *Author*

Callander

Then: 3 April 1961
During the holidays and summer months of the late 1950s and early 1960s, British Rail operated a six-car diesel set, the 'Six Lochs Rail Cruise', from Glasgow (Buchanan Street) to Oban via the Callander & Oban line and Killin branch. The train is seen at the west end of Callander station, whilst the driver and passengers wait for the signal to clear for the train to depart. The railways first reached Callander,

from Dunblane, on 1 July 1858, but the line from Callander to Killin Junction did not follow until 1 June 1870, at which time a new station serving the town was opened. It was in 1866 that the first sod was cut for the future 71-mile extension to Oban; the ultimate destination of the line did not   open until 1880.
S. Rickard

Now: 25 October 1998
Passenger services from Dunblane through Callander to Crianlarich (Lower) ceased on 1 November 1965. The line was to close completely at the same time. Today the station site at Callander is occupied by a vast car park, which was deserted at the west end on this wet October day. *Author*

Balquhidder

Then: 25 May 1957
With the Braes o'Balquhidder in the background, an amateur photographers' special from Glasgow to Killin pauses at the station on its way back to Glasgow. The train is being hauled by a couple of Stanier Class 5s, with the leading locomotive being No 45084 of Stirling. The Callander & Oban line from Callander to Killin opened on 1 June 1870. The line from Crieff and St Fillans, which joined the C&O route at Balquhidder Junction, opened from Lochearnhead on 1 May 1905 along with the station. Balquhidder was situated about three miles from the settlement it purported to serve; a halt was situated a mile further south, which was closer to the village. *BR*

Now: 25 October 1998
The line from Balquhidder to Lochearnhead closed completely on 1 October 1951. Passenger services between Callander and Crianlarich were replaced by a bus after 28 September due to a landslip in Glenogle. The line from Dunblane to Crianlarich (Lower) was to close completely on 1 November 1965. The overbridge from which the 'Then' shot was taken has long since vanished, together with everything else connected with the station. A static caravan is at the east end of the site, but otherwise it is just an open space surrounded by trees. The upgraded road passes just to the left and a road sign still proclaims 'Balquhidder Station'. *Author*

Glenoglehead

Then: 12 May 1962

Initially called 'Killin', this was the temporary terminus of the Callander & Oban line from 1 June 1870 until August 1873. Killin itself was at least four miles from the station. It was renamed Glenoglehead on 30 September 1891 and closed in December 1916, thereafter becoming Glenoglehead Crossing. It was the summit of the very steep seven-mile climb up Glen Ogle, mainly at 1 in 60, and was 941ft above sea level. On a superb summer's evening, ex-CR Single No 123 pilots ex-NBR 'Glen' No 256 *Glen Douglas* past the closed station on a returning special to Glasgow. It had travelled from Glasgow to Oban on the outward journey via the West Highland line as far as Crianlarich. *Author*

Now: 25 October 1998

Closed completely from 1 November 1965, the line through Glenoglehead was effectively closed from 28 September 1965 when a landslip forced the replacement of the remaining services by bus. The trackbed is still well defined and the station building is now two houses. The main road passes a few yards to the left. The viaduct in Glen Ogle still stands and can be seen from the main road on the hillside. *Author*

Loch Tay

Then: 3 April 1964

This picture shows the station at Loch Tay, which, by the date of this photograph, was already in private hands. In the distance can be seen the little shed which housed one locomotive, with the branch terminating in the shed. The branch from Killin Junction to Killin and Loch Tay opened on 1 April 1886. The section from Killin to Loch Tay, where a connection was made with a steamer, lost its passenger services on 9 September 1939. *I. G. Holt*

Now: 25 October 1998

The shed continued in use until 4 October 1965, shortly before the line closed completely on 1 November 1965. The old station building still stands, but is today hidden by the trees. The trackbed now forms a drive to a private house, which has been built on the site of the old shed. *Author*

Crianlarich Junction

Then: 12 May 1962

Prior to the closure of the Callander & Oban line to the east of this location, the spur between the ex-NBR and ex-CR lines was little used. The C&O line from Killin to Crianlarich opened in August 1873; it extended westwards to Dalmally on 1 April 1877. The ex-NBR line from Helensburgh to Fort William opened on 7 August 1894 and the connecting spur, through Crianlarich Glasgow Junction, opened on 20 December 1897. The signalbox which controlled the junction can be seen in the photograph, along with the West Highland line crossing the viaduct in the background. Here preserved Caledonian Single No 123 and NBR 'Glen' No 256 *Glen Douglas* head towards Oban over the connecting spur. *Author*

Killin

Then: 10 August 1960
One of the ex-CR 0-4-4Ts, No 55173, which operated the line for many years, prepares to leave the station with the 11.5am service to Killin Junction. The backdrop must have been one of the finest for any station in the country. The line from Killin Junction to Loch Tay opened on 1 April 1886, passenger services ceasing on 9 September 1939. *Author*

Now: 25 October 1998
Passenger services between Killin and Killin Junction ceased on 28 September 1965 due to the Glenogle landslip; thereafter services were operated by bus until official closure on 1 November 1965 when the line closed completely. The station at Killin has become yet another car park, with the far end now being used by the local council. *Author*

Now: 23 October 1998
The Callander & Oban line east of Crianlarich closed completely on 1 November 1965 with the exception of a short siding at Crianlarich which was retained for timber traffic. On this occasion, a train for aluminium traffic was stabled on the siding, possibly as a result of flooding on the West Highland line. As can be seen, there has been a considerable amount of rationalisation at this point. Today, services between Oban and Glasgow travel over the old C&O as far as this point and then travel over ex-NBR metals southwards. *Author*

Dalmally

Then: 12 May 1962
This view of the station shows the magnificent scenery surrounding the site to good effect. The station was in excellent condition and, at this date, was of course still staffed. Note also the cattle wagons in the siding on the right-hand side. Dalmally was the terminus of the Callander & Oban line from 1 April 1877 until the extension into Oban was completed on 30 June 1880. *Author*

Now: 23 October 1998
With the line now being controlled by Radio Electronic Token Block (RETB) signalling, the signalbox is now used by Railtrack as an office/store. The condition of the station, now unstaffed, has deteriorated considerably, with all the glass now removed from the platform awning. Class 156 No 156467 is pictured ready to depart with the 12.45 service from Oban to Glasgow (Queen Street). *Author*

Loch Awe

Then: 19 May 1961
This is another station on the line with lovely surroundings. St Rollox-allocated Class 5 No 45400 is caught departing with a down freight for Oban, with Loch Awe and Kilchourn Castle in the background. The station, situated at the northern end of Loch Awe, is the first station west of Dalmally on the section of line which opened on 30 June 1880. *M. Mensing*

Now: 23 October 1998
Loch Awe station closed on 1 November 1965, but was happily to be reopened on 10 May 1985 and remains in use. Today, trees and bushes are unfortunately blocking part of the view. A camping coach has arrived, replacing the freight wagons of 37 years ago. *Author*

Connel Ferry

Then: June 1956
This was the junction for the 27.5-mile long branch from the C&O main line to Ballachulish. The main line opened between Dalmally and Oban on 30 June 1880, with the Ballachulish line following on 21 August 1903. Here, an up service for Glasgow is seen entering the station hauled by two Stanier Class 5s, Nos 44721 and 45153. The Ballachulish branch train can be seen on the left of the picture. *Ian Allan Library (K3059)*

Now: 23 October 1998
The Ballachulish branch was to close completely on 28 March 1966, at which time passenger services over the route ceased. The station at Connel Ferry is still open, but very much reduced in size. Only one platform remains in use, which was the one used by the branch train in the 'Then' photograph. The station area and the old through platforms have now become part of the site occupied by an oil distribution company, Gleaner Oils. *Author*

Kentallen

Then: 29 July 1959
Another view of an ex-CR Class 652 0-6-0 at an intermediate station on the Ballachulish line sees No 57667 at Kentallen. This was a regular locomotive over the branch in the late 1950s. It is pictured ready to depart with the freight from Ballachulish to Oban. The line opened on 21 August 1903. Kentallen station was to close on 25 May 1953 but was reopened on 24 August of the same year. *K. R. Pirt*

Appin

Then: 27 July 1959
This was one of seven intermediate stations on the line between Connel Ferry and Ballachulish. Here we see ex-CR Class 652 0-6-0 No 57667 heading the pick-up freight back from Ballachulish towards Oban. The line to Ballachulish opened on 21 August 1903. *K. R. Pirt*

Now: 23 October 1998
Passenger services to Ballachulish ceased on 28 March 1966, at which time the line closed completely. Today, the trackbed and platforms are still extant, but all other signs of the railway have disappeared. Whilst asking directions at a local garage, the father of the owner was able to give precise instructions as he had been a porter at the station at the time of closure. *Author*

Now: 23 October 1998
As can be seen, the station site has been converted into the Holly Tree Hotel. It has been greatly extended and enjoys superb views across Loch Linnhe. This view was not taken from off the old platform edge, as that would have resulted in a view of no more than the outside wall of one of the chalets (the edge of which can be seen in the photograph), but from a position a few yards along the platform. The walls inside the hotel are graced by numerous railway photographs, although not all are from the branch. *Author*

Ballachulish

Then: 20 May 1960
The ex-CR 0-4-4Ts operated the service over the branch for many years. No 55238, still fitted with a Caledonian chimney, is pictured ready to leave. The locomotives always appeared to work chimney-first towards Oban. The station building is shown in the background. The branch opened on 21 August 1903. Steam continued on the branch after the main line had been dieselised, as it was believed that the Type 2s (later Class 27s) were too heavy for the line initially; however, in 1962 diesel traction arrived. *M. Mensing*

Now: 23 October 1998
After freight traffic over the branch ceased on 14 June 1965, the line was mainly retained for use by schoolchildren until passenger services were withdrawn on 28 March 1966. Modern houses have been built on the spot where the locomotive was standing in 1960. The station still stands behind these new buildings and is today in use as a medical centre. *Author*

Oban

Then: 12 May 1962
The station opened on 30 June 1880. It was a fine structure, primarily built of wood and the facade had a clock tower and Swiss chalet-type architecture. This impressive line-up occurred when preserved ex-CR Single No 123 and ex-NBR 'Glen' No 256 *Glen Douglas* visited the town with a special from Glasgow. Type 2 No D5352 (later No 27006) is ready to depart and Ivatt 2-6-0 No 46468 is acting as station pilot. This was one of the last active steam locomotives to operate from Oban shed, which closed later in the year. *Author*

Ballachulish shed

Then: 13 August 1960
This was a two-road shed, although only one seemed to be used regularly. Ex-CR 0-4-4T No 55224 was the branch locomotive on this occasion and is pictured outside the shed. Note the supports for the outside walls. The shed was opened with the branch in 1903 and probably fell out of use with the end of steam on the line in 1962. *Author*

Now: 23 October 1998
The shed was eventually taken over by a local garage, which used it for many years. The business has now transferred to another site, about half a mile away; whether this was because the shed has become unsafe or not is not known, but the rest of the yard is also now derelict. *Author*

Now: 23 October 1998
The roof at Oban station became unsafe and in its latter days trains were operated from outside the structure; the station was demolished at the end of March 1987 and a new station built. There are now only two platforms at Oban, but the sidings to the left are still in use. On my visit in October 1998 there were timber wagons present. A supermarket has now been built just to the right of the platform on the right-hand side. *Author*

Dundee & Arbroath Joint Railway

Built originally to the gauge of 5ft 6in — the line was converted to standard gauge with the opening of the Dundee & Perth Railway in 1847 — the Dundee & Arbroath Railway was opened on 6 October 1838. The line was extended, courtesy of the Arbroath & Forfar Railway, to Forfar on 3 January 1839. The line passed to the Scottish North Eastern Railway in 1862. The SNER was itself absorbed by the Caledonian Railway in 1866. The line's joint existence came into effect on 1 February 1880 as a result of the North British Railway's opening of the first Tay railway bridge. The old Arbroath & Forfar remained wholly owned by the Caledonian. At the Grouping in 1923 the D&A retained its joint status; it was only to lose the status with the Nationalisation of the railways in 1948 and the creation of a single Scottish Region.

In Dundee, the D&A was provided with its own terminus station — Dundee (East) — which was at the end of a short spur from Camperdown Junction. This station was to close on 5 January 1959.

Apart from the main line, the D&A also controlled the five-mile-long line from Elliot Junction to Carmyllie. This branch originated as a mineral line serving quarries in the Carmyllie area, which opened for freight only in May 1854. Operation of the line was taken over by the Scottish North Eastern Railway in February 1864. Once the joint arrangement between the Caledonian and North British railways was established in 1880, it was agreed that each company would operate the still freight-only branch in alternate years.

With the passing of the Light Railways Act in 1896, the branch was reconstituted as the Elliot Junction & Carmyllie Light Railway in 1898. Passenger services were introduced over the branch on 1 February 1900 and the branch was provided with three intermediate stations. The line, which headed effectively due north from Elliot Junction, was steeply graded.

Passenger services to Carmyllie were relatively short-lived, being suspended between 31 December 1916 and 1 February 1919 as a World War 1 economy measure before being withdrawn completely on 2 December 1929. The line then continued as a freight-only route until complete closure on 24 May 1965 except for a short spur at Elliot Junction, retained to serve a Metal Box factory, which survived until 29 July 1984.

Today, the Dundee & Arbroath Joint sees passenger and freight services between Aberdeen and Dundee; with the closure of the former Scottish North Eastern line through Forfar as a through route in the late 1960s, the D&A's importance grew and it is today an essential part of the Scottish railway network.

Elliot Junction

Then: 27 May 1960
This station is located about two miles west of Arbroath and was the point where the Carmyllie Light Railway headed north. The Dundee & Arbroath Joint Railway was controlled by the North British and Caledonian railways and provided the former's access to its otherwise isolated line from Arbroath to Kinnaber Junction and Inverbervie. The line opened from Dundee to Arbroath on 6 October 1838. The Carmyllie Light Railway, which had originally opened as a mineral line in 1854, was reopened as a Light Railway on 1 February 1900. By the date of this photograph, passenger services had already ceased, being withdrawn on 2 December 1929, but the line remained open for freight. This view was taken looking south towards the junction, with signalbox and station clearly visible. The gates controlled the level crossing just to the north of the junction. *T. G. Hepburn*

Now: 26 October 1998
The Carmyllie Light Railway was to close completely north of the Metal Box siding at Elliot Junction on 24 May 1965. The remaining spur remained until complete closure on 29 July 1984. The trackbed is still easy to follow and the level crossing gates seem to have survived. The road across the level crossing is extremely busy and a small car park has been constructed on the south side. The footbridge over the main line still survives, although Elliot Junction station itself closed on 4 September 1967. *Author*

Arbroath

Then: 3 September 1977
This is probably the most modern 'Then' photograph in the book and shows the north end of Arbroath station. A six-car rake of Class 101 DMUs painted in rail blue is seen approaching from the Aberdeen direction; the sidings adjacent are those at the north end of the station which were used to store DMUs on services which had terminated at Arbroath. The line from Dundee opened on 6 October 1838. The line was extended northwards to Colliston on 4 December 1838. The section from Arbroath northwards through Colliston to Guthrie formed part of the Caledonian; the North British line, which left the ex-CR line at St Vigeans Junction, opened, after the completion of the Tay Bridge, on 1 October 1880. It was through Arbroath and on to Montrose that the North British expresses rushed towards Aberdeen during the 'Races to the North' at the end of the 19th century. *Author*

Now: 26 October 1998
It is only relatively recently that the factory which once occupied the site behind the still extant signalbox has been demolished. Whether the site is due to be redeveloped is not known. However, its disappearance makes the view look very different as Class 158 No 158722 heads north past the signalbox with a late evening service. *Author*

Glasgow & South Western Railway

Whilst the Caledonian Railway was ultimately to form a major part of the West Coast main line between London and Glasgow through its ownership of the line through Annandale, the Glasgow & South Western was also to provide a link between Glasgow and Carlisle, this time via the supposedly easier Clydesdale route. Ironically, however, after years of competing with the CR, the G&SWR was eventually to find itself merged into its larger competitor as part of the LMSR at the Grouping.

The G&SWR was the result of a merger between the Glasgow, Paisley, Kilmarnock & Ayr Railway and the Glasgow, Dumfries & Carlisle Railway following an Act of 9 July 1847 which stated that the merger should take place upon the opening of the latter line. As such, the G&SWR came into existence on 28 October 1850. The former constituent was authorised, on 15 July 1837, to construct a railway from Ayr to Glasgow. Also authorised was the construction of branches to Dalry and Kilwinning. The main line was opened in a number of stages: from Ayr to Irvine on 5th August 1839; from Irvine to Kilwinning on 23 March 1840; from Kilwinning to Beith on 21 July 1840; and, Beith to Glasgow on 12 August 1840.

The second major constituent of the G&SWR was the Glasgow, Dumfries & Carlisle Railway. This line was authorised on 13 August 1846 to construct a line from Gretna Junction (on the Caledonian Railways main line from Carlisle northwards) via Dumfries to an end-on junction with an extension of the GPK&AR at New Cumnock (south of Kilmarnock). The line opened in three stages: from Gretna Junction to Dumfries on 23 August 1848; from Dumfries to Closeburn on 15 October 1849; and, finally, from Closeburn to New Cumnock on 28 October 1850. It was from this date that the merger with the GPK&AR became effective.

The years after 1850 were to witness considerable development. The Ayr & Dalmellington Railway opened to freight services on 15 May 1856 and to passenger on the following 7 August. The line south from Ayr opened in a number of stages: Ayr-Maybole opened to freight on 15 September 1856 and passenger services on 13 October 1856; from Maybole to Girvan, the line opened on 24 May 1860; and, finally, from Girvan to the junction with the Portpatrick & Wigtownshire Joint at Challoch Junction on 5 October 1870. Other developments in Ayrshire saw the opening of the line from Ayr to Mauchline on 1 September 1870. The line from Ardrossan to Largs opened in four stages: Ardrossan-West Kilbride (1 May 1878); West Kilbride-Fairlie (1 June 1880); Fairlie-Fairlie Pier (1 July 1882); and, finally, Fairlie Pier Junction-Largs (on 1 June 1885). In Glasgow, St Enoch station opened on 1 May 1876; the associated hotel followed on 3 July 1879. The station passed into G&SWR ownership on 29 June 1883.

The G&SWR gained access to the lucrative traffic to and from Greenock (and thus the Clyde ferries) through the Greenock & Ayrshire Railway. This line opened through to Greenock for mineral traffic on 1 September 1869 and to passenger services on 23 December. Initially, there was intense — and damaging — price competition with the CR; however, an agreement to divide the takings over the routes to Greenock meant that fares and services were restored to a sensible level. Elsewhere in Glasgow, there was considerable co-operation with the CR; there were a number of joint lines — such as the Glasgow, Barrhead & Kilmarnock Joint (which opened on 26 June 1873) and the Glasgow & Renfrew District Railway (opened on 1 June 1903 but closed to passenger services on 19 July 1926). Another of the G&SWR's Glasgow lines was one of the oldest railways in Scotland. The Paisley & Renfrew Railway was authorised as a 4ft 6in gauge

line on 21 July 1835 and opened on 3 April 1837. Initially loco-operated, horses later replaced steam. The line led a somewhat tenuous existence until acquired by the G&SWR on 31 July 1852. It was not to be regauged until 1866, with passenger services being suspended from 23 January for that purpose; it reopened as a standard gauge line on 1 May 1866. The ex-G&SWR lines inherited by the LMSR were to suffer relatively lightly during the period of the Grouping. Those lines that closed included: Annbank-Mauchline (on 4 January 1943; the line, however, was subsequently reopened and has led a somewhat checkered career since then); Ayr-Girvan (in two stages, from Ayr to Turnberry on 1 December 1930 and from Turnberry to Girvan on 3 March 1942; the section from Ayr to the holiday camp at Heads of Ayr was reopened during the summer between 1947 and 1968); and, Catrine-Mauchline (on 3 May 1943).

At Nationalisation, BR's Scottish Region assumed responsibility for the surviving ex-G&SWR lines. As elsewhere, the era of Nationalisation witnessed a gradual diminution in these lines. Much of the network serving central Ayrshire was reduced, for example. Amongst lines to close were Kilmacolm-Greenock (Princes Pier) (on 2 February 1959), Ayr-Dalmellington, Crosshouse-Irvine, Hurlford-Darvel (all on 6th April 1964), Kilmarnock-Barassie (on 3 May 1969) and Mauchline-Ayr (on 13 June 1977). The G&SWR's impressive station in Glasgow — St Enoch — was to close on 27 June 1966, but was not to be demolished for a further decade, being finally obliterated in November 1977. More recently, the Kilmacolm branch — the rump of the line to Princes Pier — via Paisley Canal closed on 10 January 1983, although the section to Paisley Canal was reopened on 28 July 1990. The closures were, however, countered to an extent by investment in the Glasgow suburban network; this work, for example, saw the electrification of the Ayrshire coast route to Fairlie and Largs.

Today, the main core of the lines inherited from the G&SWR remain operational. The route south from Ayr, following the closure of the Portpatrick & Wigtown Joint, provides Stranraer with its only link to the railway network. Further inland, the main line via Dumfries continues to offer both a passenger service for the communities along it as well as an essential diversionary route in the event of closure of the West Coast main line. Closer to Glasgow, a number of suburban lines also survive and have now been electrified.

Dumfries

Then: 13 June 1959

Dumfries has always appeared to be a well maintained station. It was an important centre, from which the 'Port Road' to Stranraer headed west, the GSWR main line ran north-south and the Caledonian line towards Lockerbie headed east. In addition, the branch to Moniaive left the main line at Cairn Valley Junction to the north of the town. All in all, Dumfries was a busy railway junction. The 'Now' shot illustrates the second station at Dumfries, which opened in March 1859. There was also a shed just to the south of the station. A WD 2-8-0 No 90640 heads south with a train from Hurlford. *R. Leslie*

Now: 25 April 1998

This view has changed little over the years, except for the removal of the centre road. This is despite the major contraction of Dumfries as a railway centre. The 'Port Road' is long gone, although a spur continued to serve Maxwelltown until the early 1990s whilst the lines to both Moniaive and Lockerbie have closed. A Strathclyde-liveried Class 156 Sprinter, No 156505, calls with the 17.30 service from Glasgow to Carlisle at 19.16. *Author*

Gretna Green

Then: 4 June 1960

The first station over the border is Gretna Green; the station here was opened as 'Gretna' on 23 August 1848 by the Glasgow, Dumfries & Carlisle Railway. The most important train of the day over the line in 1960 was the 'Thames-Clyde Express'. It is seen here passing the station headed by Class A3 No 60092 *Fairway*, which had then only just been reallocated to Leeds Holbeck. *Author*

Now: 21 May 1998

Gretna Green station closed on 6 December 1965 and freight facilities were withdrawn from the station on 3 April 1967. A new station was opened in October 1993 and, as the picture shows, the new station is about 200yd to the west of the original location. The old station still stands and I took the 'Now' photograph from the road bridge to show the new layout, rather than from the embankment where the platform used to be and where everything today would have been obscured by the bushes. *Author*

Dalbeattie

Then: 24 April 1965
This station was situated some 15 miles southwest of Dumfries on the GSWR line to Castle Douglas and Kirkcudbright. It was situated at the bottom of the 8.5-mile bank from Lochanhead. The station opened on 7 November 1859. Only two months before closure, Standard Class 4MT No 80117 arrives at the station with the 2.50pm service from Dumfries to Kirkcudbright. The line from Castle Douglas to Kirkcudbright lost its passenger services on 3 May 1965, about a month prior to the closure of the line from Dumfries to Stranraer. The locomotive is some distance from where it started life, in May 1955, at Whitby. *D. C. Smith*

Now: 26 April 1998
Like all stations on the line from Dumfries to Stranraer, passenger services ceased on 14 June 1965 at which time the line was closed completely. There is today very little to indicate that the railway used to pass here, although the trackbed could be identified in the trees in the background. The site appeared to belong to a transport company, although there was very little sign of current use on this occasion. *Author*

Castle Douglas (west end)

Then: June 1956
One of the ex-LMS Compounds allocated to Stranraer, No 41132, is pictured in the station working out its last days of service. The branch headed off right (south) to Kirkcudbright and the Portpatrick & Wigtown Joint — known as the 'Port Road' — headed west from here.
Ian Allan Library (K3070)

Castle Douglas (east end)

Then: 1 July 1961
The railway first reached Castle Douglas with the opening of the line from Dumfries on 7 November 1859. This was followed on 12 March 1861 with the opening of the 'Port Road' to Stranraer. The station became a junction with the opening of the GSWR branch to Kirkcudbright on 17 February 1864. The ex-LMS Class 2P 4-4-0s worked the Dumfries-Stranraer line for many years and here Stranraer-allocated No 40623 is pictured ready to leave with a service for Dumfries. The Kirkcudbright branch train is on the left. *Author*

Now: 26 April 1998
Passenger services over the Stranraer-Dumfries ceased on 14 June 1965 and the line was closed completely at the same time. The line to Kirkcudbright lost its passenger services on 3 May 1965 and was to close completely along with the Stranraer-Dumfries route. The east end of the station appears today to be a parking area for MacTaggart Bros transport. *Author*

Now: 26 April 1998
The railways around Castle Douglas closed completely on 14 June 1965, when passenger and freight services were withdrawn from the Stranraer-Dumfries line and freight from the Castle Douglas-Kirkcudbright line. I am afraid that today, the triumph of the motor car is complete in Castle Douglas, with the former station site now being occupied by the Ford dealer Rogerson Motors. *Author*

Tarff

Then: 16 April 1965
When this station — one of two intermediate stations between Castle Douglas and Kirkcudbright — opened on 7 March 1864, it was called 'Tarff for Gatehouse'. On 1 September 1865 it became 'Gatehouse' before becoming 'Tarff' finally on 1 August 1871. Standard Class 4MT No 76073, which went new to Dumfries and (apart from its last two months in service) spent all its life based there, is pictured arriving with the 9.25am service from Kirkcudbright to Castle Douglas. *W. G. Sumner*

Now: 26 April 1998
Passenger services ceased over the Kirkcudbright-Castle Douglas line on 3 May 1865, with freight facilities being withdrawn from the station the previous month. The line from Castle Douglas to Kirkcudbright was to close completely in June 1965. The station has been converted into a fine private house, whose owners have developed a large agricultural centre on the site. *Author*

Sanquhar

Then: 13 June 1963
Impressive power has been provided for the 5.30pm Glasgow St Enoch-Carlisle stopping train in the form of Polmadie's 'Princess Coronation' class Pacific No 46223 *Princess Alice*. This station was opened on 28 October 1850 by the Glasgow, Paisley, Kilmarnock & Ayr Railway. *D. A. McNaught*

Kirkcudbright

Then: 1 July 1961
This was the terminus of the branch from Castle Douglas. The line was opened on 7 March 1864. Stanier 2-6-2T No 40152 was working the branch on this occasion. *Author*

Now: 26 April 1998
Passenger services between Castle Douglas and Kirkcudbright ceased on 3 May 1965 and the line was to close completely the following month. Dramatic changes have occurred in the intervening 33 years and the station site is now occupied by a housing estate. The only reference point for comparison is the steeple in the background. *Author*

Now: 29 April 1998
The original station at Sanquhar closed on 6 December 1965, but was to be reopened on 27 June 1994. Looking neat and tidy on this occasion, but provided with the ubiquitous bus shelter for passenger accommodation, the station is currently served by nine trains in the up direction and eight in the down. Part of the original station still stands derelict on the left of the photograph. *Author*

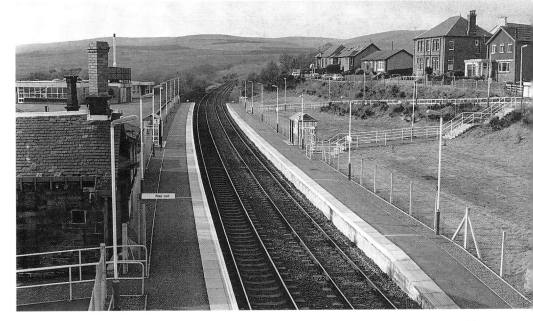

Auchinleck

Then: 27 September 1965
As can be seen this was the point where the ex-GSWR main line south towards Dumfries was joined by the line towards Muirkirk via Commondyke and Lugar headed off to the east. The lines from Kilmarnock to Auchinleck and Auchinleck to Muirkirk both opened on 9 August 1848. The station became a junction with the opening of the main line southwards to New Cumnock on 20 May 1850. Standard Class 4MT No 76092 is pictured hauling a northbound coal train over the junction from the main line into the station. *C. J. Loftus*

Now: 29 April 1998
Passenger services between Auchinleck and Muirkirk ceased on 3 July 1950 (albeit temporarily reopened between 10 September and 1 October 1951 for diverted services) and the line was subsequently to close completely. Auchinleck station was to close on 6 December 1965 but, happily, was to be reopened on 12 May 1984. All signs of the Muirkirk branch have disappeared and the former junction has been replaced by two simple through lines. *Author*

Muirkirk

Then: September 1951
Muirkirk is in a remote area, which used to be a centre of the coal mining industry. It was situated on the line from Carstairs through to Auchinleck or Cumnock. It was the point where the GSWR made an end-on connection with the ex-CR line to Carstairs. The station opened on 9 August 1848 with the opening of the line through from

Auchinleck. The Caledonian line to Douglas was opened on 1 January 1873 for freight and 1 June 1874 for passengers. The original station closed in 1896 being replaced with the station, a little to the west, illustrated here. One of the local ex-LMS Class 2P 4-4-0s, No 40575, waits alongside No 2 signalbox. *Ian Allan Library (K1289)*

Now: 29 April 1998
I found this location very difficult to sort out. There was plenty to tell me that the railway was here — in fact part of the old yard appeared to be in use as a go-kart track — but there were few people around to assist. I did, however, find a gentleman taking his grandchild for a walk who said he used to work at the station but still wasn't sure where the signalbox stood. The owner of the house told me that this was the correct place to stand for the 'Now' picture, but I am still not absolutely sure. Passenger services over the former GSWR line to the west of Muirkirk ceased on 10 September 1951, but those over the ex-CR line to Lanark survived until 5 October 1964. The line was to close completely north of Muirkirk at the same time. The line south of Muirkirk closed completely on 7 February 1969 (although a special operated over the route later that year before it was dismantled). *Author*

Newmilns

Then: 3 April 1964
This station was situated on the cross-country line westwards from Kilmarnock, which made an end-on junction with the CR line from Stonehouse at County Boundary Junction (just to the east of Loudonhall). The line opened from Galston to Newmilns on 20 May 1850; the route was extended from Newmilns to Darvel on 1 June 1896. Just before the withdrawal of passenger services, the evening parcels train from Darvel is pictured leaving the station behind Standard Class 4MT No 80024. *David C. Smith*

Now: 29 April 1998
Passenger services were withdrawn between Hurlford and Darvel via Newmilns on 6 April 1964 and the line was closed completely on 6 July 1964. The railway area has now been fully redeveloped and a company called Vesuvius Refractories now occupies the site. I have deliberately taken this 'Now' photograph from an old road bridge over the trackbed as it shows so much more than would have been visible by recreating precisely the angle of the original photograph. *Author*

Catrine

Then: April 1964

This was the terminus of a branch line which left the ex-GSWR main line at Brackenhill Junction, between Auchinleck and Mauchline. Passenger services over the line were introduced from 1 September 1903. However, these lasted a relatively short time, being withdrawn on 1 January 1917. Services were reinstated but were again to succumb, this time on 3 May 1943. Thereafter the line remained open for freight services and here Stanier Class 5 No 45497 is pictured at the terminus with the daily freight towards Ayr. *Derek Cross*

Now: 29 April 1998

Freight services to Catrine continued until 6 July 1964 when the branch from Brackenhill Junction closed completely. The area has now been landscaped and virtually nothing remains of the railway other than the bridge from which this photograph was taken. *Author*

Kilmarnock (north end)

Then: May 1955
Kilmarnock was one of the most important centres on the GSWR, with lines radiating in every direction. Railways reached the town early with the Kilmarnock & Troon Railway opening from St Marnocks Depot in Kilmarnock to Troon Harbour on 6 July 1812. The original station was replaced on 4 April 1843 by a second station owned by the Glasgow, Paisley, Kilmarnock & Ayr Railway. This only lasted until 20 July 1846 when the present station opened. This view is at the north end with one of the well-kept Hulford Class 2P 4-4-0s No 40573 waiting to leave on a local to Glasgow St Enoch, with a dirty Carlisle Kingmoor-allocated Class 5, No 45281, in the background on a Dumfries-Glasgow train. *Ian Allan Library (K2593)*

Now: 29 April 1998
The station is currently in a sorry state of repair, as one is able to see in this picture. The old up main line platform still exists but appeared to see little use, with the buildings having been demolished. The old down through road has been removed and the other lines have been signalled for bi-directional working. On this occasion, Class 156 Sprinter No 156467 was in the north bay prior to forming the 13.50 to Glasgow Central. *Author*

Lugton

Then: 25 June 1956
Caledonian '439' class 0-4-4T No 55203 has just arrived at the station with the branch train from Beith. Note the amount of coal in the bunker; I am surprised that most of it didn't fall off! The station opened on 27 March 1871 along with the Glasgow, Barrhead & Kilmarnock Railway route as far south as Stewarton (the line was extended from Stewarton to Kilmarnock on 26 June 1873 at which time the Lugton-Beith branch was also opened); the GB&KR was a joint line controlled by the GSWR and CR. There was also an ex-CR station at Lugton, but this lasted only until 1932. *G. H. Robin*

Crosshouse Junction

Then: 6 May 1948
This was the junction to the west of Kilmarnock, where the line split to Dalry in the north and Dreghorn in the west. The station was opened here by the Glasgow, Paisley, Kilmarnock & Ayr Railway on 1 September 1872. The line from Dalry to Kilmarnock opened on 4 April 1843 whilst that from Crosshouse to Dreghorn followed on 22 May 1848. This picture was taken looking east and shows an immaculate local 4-4-0 No 40644 passing the junction with a service from Kilmarnock to Ardrossan. *G. H. Robin*

Now: 29 April 1998
Today, only the trackbed remains, nature having taken over. The line from Crosshouse to Dreghorn lost its passenger services on 6 April 1964 and was to close completely on 11 October 1965. Crosshouse station was to close on 18 April 1966 (at which time local passenger services from Dalry to Kilmarnock were withdrawn). The line from Kilmarnock to Dalry was to lose its final through passenger services on 22 October 1973 and was to close completely at the same time. *Author*

Now: 29 April 1998
The signalbox still exists as this is one of the crossing points on the single-track section south from Barrhead. All traces, however, of the station, which closed on 7 November 1966, have disappeared. The branch to Beith lost its passenger services on 5 November 1962 but remains open for freight as far as a depot at Giffen. *Author*

Beith Town

Then: August 1952
Beith had two stations, one on the GSWR main line to Kilwinning (which closed on 4 June 1951) and Beith Town, which was the terminus of the branch from Barrmill Junction. The line opened on 26 June 1873 as part of the Glasgow, Barrhead & Kilmarnock Joint Railway (which was controlled by the GSWR and the CR). At this date the service was being run by a Fairburn 2-6-4T No 42122. In addition to the station and yard, there was also a small engine shed for the branch locomotive. *Ian Allan Library (K1587)*

Now: 29 April 1998
Although operated by railbuses latterly, even these economies were not enough to save the branch, which lost its passenger services on 5 November 1962 and was to close completely between Beith and Barrmill Junction on 5 October 1964. A housing estate now occupies all the railway land. The stationmaster's house survives and is now owned by a local railway enthusiast whose help in taking this 'Now' photograph was very much appreciated. *Author*

Johnstone

Then: 8 September 1959
This station was opened by the Glasgow, Paisley, Kilmarnock & Ayr Railway on 21 July 1840 when the line from Paisley to Howwood opened. It was known as 'Johnstone' from opening, but became 'Johnstone High' on 18 June 1951. A Fairburn 2-6-4T, No 42123, is shown at the station heading a Glasgow St Enoch-Largs express. *G. H. Robin*

Now: 29 April 1998
The station has reverted to 'Johnstone' again and not a lot has altered in the past 40 years with the exception of some new houses on the right which appear to have been built on the old yard and of course electrification. The platform canopy has also gone. The line through Johnstone saw electrified services inaugurated on 29 September 1986. One of the Strathclyde Class 318 EMUs, No 318264, arrives with the 11.45 Glasgow Central-Largs service. *Author*

Houston & Crosslee

Then: 16 July 1955
Initially called simply 'Houston' when it first opened on 1 January 1874, this station saw several name changes over the years with the addition or deletion of '& Crosslee'. Here Standard Class 4MT No 80009 is pictured working the 10.13am Greenock Prince's Pier-Glasgow St Enoch service. *W. A. Camwell*

Now: 29 April 1998
Following the cessation of services through to Prince's Pier, Kilmacolm became the terminus of the branch from Cart Junction. Although most other Glasgow suburban services became electrified, that to Kilmacolm remained diesel-operated. The branch was to close completely on 10 January 1983. Today, part of the platform edge survives and the trackbed appears to have been converted into a cycleway and footpath. Otherwise nature has taken over in a major way. *Author*

Glasgow (St Enoch)

Then: 11 April 1966

This fine Glasgow & South Western terminus never seemed to receive the same attention as Glasgow (Central), probably because it didn't have the glamour trains like the 'Royal Scot' and the 'Caledonian'. Nevertheless, there were the 'Thames Clyde Express', the London sleeper and the Stranraer boat train; in fact there was probably a greater variety of motive power than at Central. In the latter years of steam, ex-LMS and ex-LNER Pacifics were seen virtually on a daily basis and there was a frequent sight of double-heading with Class 2P 4-4-0s. The station opened on 17 October 1876. Here a Standard 2-6-4T, No 80054 with express headcode but with non-corridor coaching stock, heads out of Platform No 1 round the sharp curve with a relief train to Ayr. The building visible behind the locomotive's exhaust used to house the G&SWR administrative headquarters. *Derek Cross*

Now: 28 October 1998

The closure of St Enoch on 27 June 1966 no doubt came as a considerable surprise to many. This is probably the most dramatic change of any location featured in the book. There is nothing to indicate that there was once a main line terminus on the site. The St Enoch shopping centre is impressive, but like most shopping centres it seems to lack atmosphere and character. The umbrellas indicate that, once again in 1998, it was pouring down in Glasgow. *Author*

Paisley (Gilmour Street)

Then: May 1958
Polmadie-allocated Fairburn 2-6-4T No 42056 passes through the station with a local train to Gourock. The train will turn right at this point and follow the ex-CR line. The station opened on 14 July 1840 with the opening of the Glasgow & Paisley Joint Railway to the station. From Gilmour Street westwards, the line was ultimately to form part of the G&SWR; the future Caledonian line towards Greenock opened in March 1841. The station illustrated here was the result of later rebuilding. *Ian Allan Library (K3676)*

Now: 28 October 1998
Strathclyde Class 318 No 318263 sets off from the station with the 09.59 departure for Largs over the ex-G&SWR line. The station layout has altered little over the years, although the platform awnings have been replaced and electric services have arrived. *Author*

Renfrew Wharf

Then: 8 September 1966/June 1956
In spite of appearances, when the first of these two 'Then' photographs was taken, passenger services were still operating. The line originally opened — as the Paisley & Renfrew Railway — on 3 April 1837. The original purpose of the line was to provide a connection for travellers to and from the many vessels that plied along the River Clyde. It was originally 4ft 6in in gauge and passed to the G&SWR in mid-1852; it was not until 1 August 1866, however, that the line was converted to standard gauge, services having been suspended earlier in the year. The River Clyde can just be seen beyond the buffer stops. Also visible is Yoker power station. The second of the 'Then' photographs shows one of the Corkerhill-allocated Class 2P 4-4-0s, No 40596, ready to depart for St Enoch. *C. C. Thornburn/ Ian Allan Library (K3055)*

Now: 28 October 1998
Passenger services were withdrawn between Renfrew Wharf and Arkleston Junction on 5 June 1967. The section to Renfrew Wharf (Buchanan power station) was to close completely on 5 June 1978. The site presented a very sorry spectacle on my visit. It was fenced off, so I had to take the picture from a slightly different angle. The area used to be occupied by a chemical company. *Author*

Bellahouston/Dumbreck

Then: 18 September 1954
The station originally opened on 1 July 1885. Closed on 1 January 1917, during World War 1, it was subsequently reopened. Here ex-CR 0-4-4T No 55211 leaves with the 5.46pm service for Paisley (West) from St Enoch. The picture was taken from the west end of the platforms with the station buildings visible in the background. The train recorded here was, in fact, the last scheduled train to call at the station as passenger facilities were withdrawn officially from the station on 20 September 1954. *J. L. Stevenson*

Now: 22 October 1998
This was a particularly difficult location to sort out. The old station had been completely demolished although the roadside station building can just be made out above the Class 101 DMU; this is the same building that is visible above the last coach in the 'Then' photograph. A new station called Dumbreck opened on 28 July 1990 about 200yd to the west of the old station. Between the site of the old and new stations, the M77 has been built, so this picture was taken off the east end of Dumbreck station platform and shows the DMU passing the point occupied by the Caley tank in the 'Then' shot. A long telephoto lens was necessary to obtain the picture. *Author*

Kilmacolm

Then: 23 May 1964
This station was situated on the branch from Cart Junction to Greenock Prince's Pier, which was opened by the Greenock & Ayrshire Railway to freight on 1 September 1869 and to passengers on the following 23 December. The G&AR became part of the GSWR in 1872. Here a DMU awaits departure with a service for Glasgow St Enoch. By the date of this photograph, local passenger services between Kilmacolm and Prince's Pier had been withdrawn, although boat trains continued to operate.
J. Spencer Gilks

Paisley Canal

Then: 16 April 1960
Corkerhill (67A)-allocated BR Standard
Class 4MT No 76092 rolls into the old
station with the 2.11pm service to
Glasgow (St Enoch). The line opened on
1 July 1885. *J. Brown*

Now: 28 October 1998
The line through Paisley Canal latterly
formed part of the dieselised line to
Kilmacolm. This route was closed on
3 January 1983. The line remained open
for freight east of this point and, on
28 July 1990, the line from Shields
Junction to a new station called Paisley
Canal was located 250yd east of the old
station. There is, however, very little to
indicate that a railway ever passed this
way. The trackbed is now utilised as a
footpath and cycleway, whilst the
surrounding area has been heavily
redeveloped. *Author*

Now: 29 April 1998
Boat trains ceased to operate to Prince's
Pier on 30 November 1965 and the line
was to close completely beyond
Kilmacolm on 26 September 1966.
Thereafter Kilmacolm became the
terminus of the branch. DMU services
over the line were to survive until
10 January 1983 when the line from
Cart Junction was closed completely.
The station building still exists but it has
been extensively extended and altered.
At the time of the photograph, the
building was undergoing further
alterations and was possibly a
pub/restaurant. *Author*

Greenock Prince's Pier

Then: 18 April 1949
When it was opened to passengers on 23 December 1869, the first station served Greenock Albert Harbour, but with reconstruction and relocation (300yd to the west) in 1894 — the new station opened on 25 May of that year — the station became known as Greenock Prince's Pier. Here Fairburn 2-6-4T No 2190, still bearing its original LMS number, is pictured ready to depart for Glasgow. *J. F. Henton*

Now: 28 April 1998
Local passenger services over the line beyond Kilmacolm ceased on 2 February 1959 but boat trains continued to serve Prince's Pier until 30 November 1965. The line was to close completely on 26 September 1966 between Prince's Pier and Kilmacolm. The site is now a container base for Associated British Ports. My thanks are due to the manager who allowed me on to the site to take the photograph. At the time of my visit the terminal was not rail connected. *Author*

Dalry

Then: 11 September 1959
This used to be a busy location, where the main line from Glasgow split, with lines heading to Kilwinning and Kilmarnock. Here BR Standard Class 5MT No 73122 heads south at the head of a rake of empty coal wagons. The station was provided with four tracks as well as sidings. The GSWR main line from Kilwinning to Beith opened on 10 July 1840 and the route from Dalry to Kilmarnock followed on 4 April 1843. *Author*

Glengarnock

Then: 14 July 1959
Class 2 4-4-0 No 40688 calls at the station, one of the intermediate stations between Kilbarchan and Dalry, with a service from Glasgow St Enoch and Kilmarnock. The station was originally known as 'Glengarnock & Kilbirnie' when it opened on 21 July 1840; it became 'Glengarnock' on 1 June 1905. *G. H. Robin*

Now: 29 April 1998
Strathclyde Class 318 No 318262 calls at the station with the 09.15 service from Glasgow Central to Ardrossan Town. Apart from the electrification and the new footbridge — plus a few more trees on the right-hand side — little has changed here over the past 40 years. *Author*

Now: 29 April 1998
The line from Dalry to Kilmarnock lost its last through passenger services on 22 October 1973, with local services having been withdrawn on 18 April 1966. This line was to close completely with the withdrawal of the last through services on 22 October 1973. The number of tracks has been reduced to two and the line electrified, but the location remains a busy one, with services to and from the Ayrshire coast. Here Strathclyde Class 318 No 318265 rushes by nonstop with the 08.45 service from Glasgow Central to Largs, where it will arrive at 09.44. *Author*

West Kilbride

Then: 11 September 1959
Ardrossan-allocated Fairburn 2-6-4T
No 42209 leaves the station with the
1.15pm service from Largs to Glasgow
St Enoch. The station opened on 1 May
1878 when, until the opening of the line
to Fairlie on 1 June 1880, West Kilbride
was the terminus of the line from
Ardrossan. *Author*

Now: 28 April 1998
The 12.53 service from Largs to
Glasgow Central leaves the station
formed of Class 318 unit No 318250.
Note that the line on the right is not
electrified; at this point, the two lines
are separate — the one on the left is
electrified for the services to and from
Largs whilst the one on the right is for
the freight service to and from the
terminal at Hunterston. *Author*

Fairlie

Then: August 1959
Known over the years as 'Fairlie Town', 'Fairlie High' and 'Fairlie', this station was opened — as a terminus — on 1 June 1880; the line was extended north to Fairlie Pier on 1 July 1882. Here, Stanier Class 5 No 45164 calls with a local train from Largs to Glasgow St Enoch. *Ian Allan Library*

Now: 28 April 1998
The station has today been reduced to a single platform. Electrification — inaugurated over the line to Largs on 19 January 1987 — has seen the elimination of the old southbound platform and the footbridge. Class 318 EMU No 318262 calls with the 12.45 service from Glasgow Central to Largs. Just to the left of the platform is the siding which handles the nuclear flask traffic. *Author*

Largs

Then: 11 September 1959
This view shows Fairburn 2-6-4T No 42209 leaving the station with the 1.15pm service to Glasgow St Enoch. The station was opened by the GSWR on 1 June 1885 when the line to Fairlie Pier Junction was extended northwards. As can be seen, at this time the station was well provided with platforms to cope with the summer traffic of holidaymakers who flocked to the Ayrshire coast in the summer months. *Author*

Now: 28 April 1998
Largs remains the terminus of the branch from Holm Junction; the bulk of the route is now singled, although there is a parallel line as far as the port at Hunterston. The service to Glasgow Central over the electrified line is hourly and here Class 318 No 318262 is seen leaving with the 13.53 service to Central. The supermarket on the right is a relatively recent arrival on the scene. *Author*

Stevenston

Then: 4 April 1959
This station is situated on the ex-GSWR line from Kilwinning to Ardrossan (and thence to Largs). The line opened at this point on 27 July 1840. Local Class 2P 4-4-0 No 40667 calls at the station at the head of a Glasgow St Enoch-Largs service. *G. H. Robin*

Ardrossan Harbour

Then: 7 September 1961
Ex-CR McIntosh Class 3F 0-6-0T
No 56282 is seen shunting at the station;
to emphasise the arrival of the new age,
note also the diesel shunter (later
Class 08) in the background. The
railway first served the new harbour at
Ardrossan on 27 July 1840. There were
two piers at Ardrossan: Winton Pier,
which was served by the GSWR, and
Montgomerie Pier, which was served by
the CR. The latter was opened on
30 May 1890 and was to survive until
6 May 1968. *R. G. Hobbs*

Now: 28 April 1998
Strathclyde PTE relocated the station
slightly to the east and opened a new
platform on 19 January 1987.
Strathclyde Class 318 EMU No 318270
is pictured arriving at the new station on
the 11.15 service from Glasgow Central.
The old footbridge has vanished, hence
the track level viewpoint. There are
currently around five arrivals and
departures each day; some connect with
Caledonian MacBrayne ferries to
Brodick. The line was electrified on
24 November 1986. *Author*

Now: 28 April 1998
Although all the old station buildings
have been demolished and been replaced
by the ubiquitous bus shelter, passenger
services survive on the ex-GSWR route.
Slightly further inland, the town was
also served by an ex-CR line, but this
line closed some 30 years ago. Also a
casualty of progress is the footbridge,
but more positive is the arrival of
electrification (inaugurated on
24 November 1986). *Author*

Kilwinning

Then: Undated (early 1960s)
There used to be two stations here, one serving the GSWR and the second on the ex-CR line to Ardrossan. This view, looking north, shows the ex-GSWR station and Standard Class 4MT No 76099 passing with a local freight. The lines to the left form the route towards Ardrossan, whilst the locomotive is heading over the lines southwards towards Irvine, which opened on 23 March 1840. The line from Kilwinning north towards Beith opened on 10 July 1840. The line from Beith through Kilwinning to Ayr was opened under the auspices of the Glasgow, Paisley, Kilmarnock & Ayr Railway, which was authorised on 15 July 1837. *P. J. Sharpe*

Now: 28 April 1998
The station has been completely modernised, with good parking facilities for passengers requiring the frequent services to and from Glasgow, Ayr and Largs. Class 318 EMU No 318250 approaches the station with the 09.30 from Glasgow Central to Ayr. *Author*

Troon Old station (avoiding line)

Then: 4 July 1959
This was the site of the original Glasgow, Paisley, Kilmarnock & Ayr Railway station, which opened on 5 August 1839. It was closed on 2 May 1892 when it was replaced by a second station nearer the town on a realigned route. Here the 5.10pm Glasgow St Enoch-Stranraer express passes the disused platforms headed by 'Clan' class Pacific No 72009 *Clan Stewart*. *G. H. Robin*

Barassie

Then: 7 July 1954
This is the point where the original Glasgow, Paisley, Kilmarnock & Ayr Railway meets the line from Kilmarnock. The line from Kilmarnock to Troon opened on 6 July 1812, whilst the section of the GPKAR, between Ayr and Irvine, opened on 5 August 1839. The Kilmarnock & Troon was horse-operated until it was taken over by the GPKAR and regauged for locomotive operation in the 1840s. South of the station, the Troon avoiding line branched off the original line serving Troon. Here ex-CR 0-6-0 No 57355 heads south with a train consisting of two guard vans. *G. H. Robin*

Now: 28 April 1998
Passenger services over the line to Kilmarnock were withdrawn on 3 May 1969, although they were reinstated for through services on 5 May 1975. There is, however, now no platform on the Kilmarnock side of the station and the route eastwards has been singled. It is now not possible to stand in exactly the same location as a new road overbridge has been constructed a few yards to the north, which would have completely obscured the view. Class 156 Sprinter No 156514 rounds the curve from Kilmarnock forming the 08.28 service from Glasgow Central to Stranraer; the 101 miles will take 2hr 43min. *Author*

Now: 28 April 1998
The Troon avoiding line — Barassie Junction-Lochgreen Junction — lost its passenger services, with the exception of one working, on 18 April 1966 and later closed completely as a through route. The line has now been converted into a long siding from Barassie Junction, which terminates about 0.25 mile north of the old station. Today the trackbed still exists as does the old station house; however, I was told that the site was shortly to be redeveloped. *Author*

Troon

Then: 4 July 1959
This is the second station, which opened on 2 May 1892. Here Fairburn-designed 2-6-4T No 42059 is pictured about to call at the head of a Glasgow (St Enoch)-Girvan train. *G. H. Robin*

Now: 27 April 1998
Little has changed at Troon over the past 40 years, with the exception of the arrival of electrified services. Electrification was inaugurated over the line through Troon on 29 September 1986. As can be seen, the station is today well kept and it is interesting to note how carefully the original station infrastructure was adapted to accommodate the electric services. Here Class 318 EMU No 318253 is caught entering the station with the 19.00 Glasgow Central-Ayr service. *Author*

Prestwick

Then: 28 March 1959
An Ayr-Glasgow St Enoch stopping train arrives at the station headed by Hughes 'Crab' 2-6-0 No 42808. The station originally opened on 5 August 1839, but was to close and reopen twice between then and 1846. *G. H. Robin*

Troon (south)

Then: 11 September 1959
Caledonian Class 2F 0-6-0 No 57274,
one of a class designed by Drummond,
ambles along the Ayrshire coast, past the
golf courses with a short northbound
freight. This stretch of line was
originally part of the Glasgow, Paisley,
Kilmarnock & Ayr Railway, which was
authorised on 15 July 1837 and opened
between Ayr and Irvine on 5 August
1839. *G. W. Morrison*

Now: 27 April 1998
Other than the electrification — which
was inaugurated on 29 September 1986
— and the growth of the gorse, very
little has changed here over the years.
Strathclyde Class 318 EMU No 318260
is recorded heading north in superb
evening sunlight. *Author*

Now: 27 April 1998
The 17.30 from Glasgow Central to Ayr
calls at the station. The goods yard to
the left has gone as well as the line on
the right. Other than these losses — and
the arrival of the electric services —
little else has altered here over four
decades. *Author*

Newton on Ayr

Then: 11 September 1959
Located between Prestwick and Ayr, this station is situated on the section of the Glasgow, Paisley, Kilmarnock & Ayr Railway which opened on 5 August 1839. Here Standard Class 4MT No 80024, allocated to Corkerhill shed, calls at the station with an express from Glasgow St Enoch. *Author*

Now: 27 April 1998
The station is now unstaffed — which is reflected in its condition — but is otherwise largely unchanged except for the arrival of electric services. Class 318 No 318267 calls with the 16.30 service from Glasgow Central to Ayr. *Author*

Ayr

Then: 22 June 1961
Local Hughes-designed 'Crab' 2-6-0
No 42809 works wrong line through the
station heading south with a rake of
empty coal wagons. The first station at
Ayr opened, with the first section of the
Glasgow, Paisley, Kilmarnock & Ayr
Railway, on 5 August 1839. This was
replaced by a second station, called 'Ayr
Townhead', which opened in 1857 and
which lasted until 12 January 1886,
when it was replaced by the third station
— the location illustrated here — 300yd
to the south. *S. Rickard*

Now: 27 April 1998
As can be seen the station area has been
modernised with the arrival of electric
services and the appearance of colour
light signalling, although elsewhere
there has been some rationalisation of
track. Strathclyde Class 156 Sprinter
No 156502 arrives at the station forming
the 12.37 Newcastle-Stranraer service.
This journey, at 229 miles, must be
amongst the longest in the country
undertaken by the class. *Author*

Annbank Junction

Then: 27 July 1964
A special from Manchester to Largs passes the closed station — which was situated about three miles east of Ayr — headed by Carlisle Kingmoor-based 'Clan' class Pacific No 72007 *Clan MacIntosh*. This was the point where the lines to Mauchline, on the GSWR main line, and Cumnock, on the cross-country route towards Muirkirk, divided. The line from Ayr to Mauchline opened on 1 September 1870; the station became a junction with the opening of the line to Cronberry on 11 June 1872 (freight) and 1 July 1872 (passengers). By the date of this photograph, regular passenger services through Annbank on both lines had ceased. The line from Annbank to Mauchline lost its passenger services on 4 January 1943 (although they were temporarily reinstated during September 1951 for diverted services between Edinburgh and Ayr via Muirkirk); the line between Annbank and Muirkirk saw passenger services cease on 10 September 1951 and, finally, the section between Ayr and Mauchline followed on 1 October 1951 (at which time services were again withdrawn from the line to Mauchline).
Derek Cross

Now: 27 April 1998
The line on the left still continues through to Mauchline, whilst that on the right now terminates at Killoch Colliery, which is at Ochiltree. The junction has seen quite an increase in traffic over the past few years. Note that the coal waste heap in the background has been reduced considerably over the past 34 years. Through passenger services over the Ayr-Mauchline route were reinstated on 14 June 1965 when boat train services were diverted from the 'Port Road'. Regular passenger services again ceased on 13 June 1977. *Author*

Dalmellington

Then: July 1955
This was the terminus of the branch which leaves the Ayr-Girvan line at Dalrymple Junction. The line opened for freight on 15 May 1856 and to passenger services on 7 August 1856. Here, ex-LMS Class 2P 4-4-0 No 40572 is ready to depart with a service to Ayr.
Ian Allan Library (K2630)

Hollybush

Then: 28 March 1959
This station was situated on the Dalrymple Junction-Dalmellington branch, and was the only intermediate station between Dalrymple and Holehouse, where a line ran northeast towards Ochiltree. The Ayr & Dalmellington Railway opened for freight traffic on 15 May 1856 and to passenger services on the following 7 August. One of the Standard Class 3MT 2-6-0s allocated to the area, No 77017, is pictured arriving at the station with a service from Dalmellington to Kilmarnock.
G. H. Robin

Now: 27 April 1998
Passenger services over the line ceased on 6 April 1964; freight facilities had been withdrawn from the station some four years earlier. The line is still used by traffic to and from the Chalmerston open cast coal site, which is situated about three miles west of Dalmellington.
Author

Now: 27 April 1998
Passenger services over the Dalmellington branch ceased on 6 April 1964 and the section between Dalmellington and the colliery at Waterside was to close completely on 6 July 1964. The area recorded in the 'Then' shot has been landscaped over the past 34 years, but behind me a school has been built on part of the old railway property. *Author*

Heads of Ayr

Then: July 1958
This station was situated on the line which ran from Alloway Junction, to the south of Ayr, along the coast to Girvan. Here ex-LMS Class 2P 4-4-0 No 40610 is pictured arriving with a train from Ayr. The uniforms of the day are well illustrated by the Stationmaster and porter on the platform. The line between Alloway and Girvan opened on 17 May 1906 under the auspices of the Maidens & Dunure Light Railway. It closed to passenger services between Alloway and Turnberry on 1 December 1930, although services were reinstated temporarily between 4 July 1932 and 31 May 1933. The opening of a Butlins holiday camp at Heads of Ayr led to passenger services being reinstated between Alloway Junction and Heads of Ayr on 17 May 1947. Passenger services between Turnberry and Girvan ceased, never to restart, on 2 March 1942. The line south of Heads of Ayr closed completely on 28 February 1955. *Ian Allan Library (K3791)*

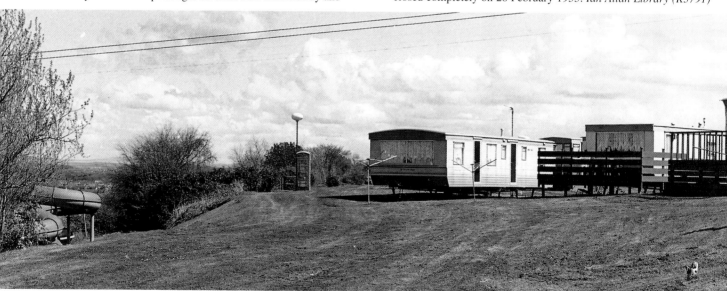

Now: 27 April 1998
The reinstated passenger service to Heads of Ayr ceased on 16 September 1968 and the remains of the Maidens & Dunure Light Railway closed completely. The change has been dramatic over the past 30 years. The railway has now been absorbed into the holiday complex. My thanks are due to the staff for allowing me on to the premises to take this picture. *Author*

90

Maybole

Then: 6 August 1960

This station is situated about halfway between Ayr and Girvan, at the summit of the line between the two towns. The first station opened here in 1856 — on 15 September to freight and on 13 October for passenger services — with the completion of the Ayr & Maybole Railway. The station was replaced on 24 May 1860 when the Maybole & Girvan Railway opened its line southwards. A Stranraer-Glasgow St Enoch express calls at the station double-headed by Stanier Class 5 No 45036 and BR Standard Class 5MT No 73100. *G. H. Robin*

Now: 27 April 1998

Today only one platform remains in use; this is more than adequate for the two-car sprinters which now form the regular services over the line to Girvan. Goods facilities were withdrawn from the station on 5 April 1965. The 11.43 Stranraer-Glasgow Central service calls at the station, worked by Class 156 No 156512. *Author*

Kilberran

Then: 15 August 1959
This is the next station south from Maybole on the line towards
Girvan and opened on 24 May 1860. Here a freight, headed by
Hughes 'Crab' 2-6-0 No 42809, heads north through the station.
G. H. Robin

Now: 27 April 1998
The line has been singled to the south, but the signals show that a
loop has been installed to the north; this is controlled by the
signalbox which also controls the level crossing from where this
photograph was taken. Kilberran station closed on 6 September 1965;
freight facilities had finished a year earlier. The station buildings are
still extant to the left of the photograph. *Author*

Barrhill

Then: 28 May 1964
This extremely remote station is 74 miles from Glasgow and is today the main crossing point between Girvan and Challoch Junction, near Dunragit. It is situated half-way up the very steep eight-mile climb; the gradient runs at up to 1 in 67 to the summit at milepost 16½. A Woodworkers' Union special, headed by Class 5 No 45164 and Standard Class 5 No 73124, waits for a Glasgow-bound train to pass. The Girvan & Portpatrick Railway, from Girvan to Challoch Junction, opened on 5 October 1877, at which time the station at Barrhill also opened; in its early years the station had a precarious existence — it had closed and reopened twice by 1886. *Derek Cross*

Now: 27 April 1998
Class 156 Sprinter No 156512, on the 08.28 Glasgow Central-Stranraer service, waits for the 10.00 Stranraer-Newcastle train to arrive. The latter had connected at Stranraer with the 07.00 ferry from Belfast. The station is still staffed; on this occasion all the duties were being carried out by the signalwoman. The station and signalbox remain intact from 34 years ago, although the prominent water tower has disappeared. *Author*

Great North of Scotland Railway

Of the five main line Scottish railways, the Great North of Scotland was the smallest. The company's origins date back to 1844 and a parliamentary Act allowing for the construction of the line from Aberdeen to Inverness was passed two years later.

The first section of the future GNoSR to open in Aberdeen was, however, the first part of the Ballater branch from Ferryhill to Banchory, which opened on 8 September 1853. The first part of the main line proper, from Kittybrewster to Huntly, opened on 12 September 1854. On 24 September 1855 this line was extended from Kittybrewster to Aberdeen (Waterloo); this line, however, retained its passenger services only until 4 November 1867 when the line to the joint station was opened. The main line was completed through to Keith, and a junction with the Highland Railway, on 10 October 1856.

Apart from the main line, the GNoSR possessed a network of secondary routes, many of which served the fishing ports of north and northeast Scotland. Of the branches, the most famous was probably that to Ballater, which was to become a regular haunt of royalty as it served the estate at Balmoral. This line was opened, as noted to Banchory, in 1853; it was extended to Aboyne on 2 December 1859 and thence to Ballater on 17 October 1866.

From Dyce, routes ran to Fraserburgh and Peterhead. The first section, from Dyce to Maud Junction and Mintlaw opened on 18 July 1861. The line to Mintlaw was extended to Peterhead on 3 July 1862 and from Maud to Fraserburgh on 24 April 1865. Two late extensions saw a branch open from Ellon (on the Peterhead line) to Boddam on 2 August 1896 and from Fraserburgh to St Combs on 1 July 1903. The former line served Cruden Bay, where the GNoSR

Aberdeen South

Then: 28 May 1930
This fine picture shows ex-GNoSR Class P (LNER Class D43) 4-4-0 No 6812 ready to leave on a train to Ballater. Three of this class were built by Robert Stephenson in 1890 and remained in service until the late 1930s. The joint station in Aberdeen, used by the Caledonian, the North British and the Great North of Scotland railways, opened on 4 November 1867; the new station replaced the earlier stations at Waterloo and Guild Street. In the 1950s and early 1960s it was possible to see Pacifics inherited from both the LMS and the LNER at the station. *H. C. Casserley*

operated an hotel; the hotel was linked to the railway by a GNoSR-owned electric tramway, which operated from June 1899 until services were suspended as a result of World War 2 in March 1941.

Heading further along the main line, Kintore was the junction for the branch to Alford; this opened on 21 March 1859. Inverurie was the location of the GNoSR's workshops; it was also the point where the short Old Meldrum branch headed northwards; this opened on 1 July 1856. Inveramsay, the next station heading westwards, was the junction for the long straggling branch to Macduff; this opened in three stages — from Inveramsay to Turriff on 5 September 1857, thence to Gellymill on 4 June 1860 and finally to Macduff on 1 July 1872. From Grange and Cairnie — where there was a triangular junction — the coastal route towards Elgin headed northwards. The first section of this line, the branch from Elgin to Lossiemouth, opened on 10 August 1852 — the first part of the future GNoSR to see public services. The coastal route diverged from this branch just to the north of Elgin. The next section was that from Grange to Portsoy, which opened on 30 July 1859, at which time the short branch from Tillynaught to Banff was also opened. The route was then opened from Portsoy to Tochineal on 1 April 1884. The section from Garmouth towards Elgin followed on 12 April 1884, with the final section, that from Garmouth to Tochineal, opening on 5 April 1886.

Apart from the coastal route, the GNoSR was also able to gain access to Elgin through an inland route. The first section of this line to open, from Rothin to Dandaleith, opened on 23 December 1858; this route was connected to the Highland line at Orton by a short-lived route which was to close in 1866. The line from Elgin to Rothin opened on 30 December 1861. From the east, the line from Keith to Dufftown opened on 21 December 1862. The line was extended through from Dufftown to Dandaleith with a branch from Craigellachie to Aberlour on 1 July 1863. The line from Aberlour was extended southwards via Grantown on Spey to meet with the Highland Railway at Abernethy on 11 July 1863.

At the Grouping, the GNoSR was to pass, along with the North British Railway, to the LNER. The period of the Grouping was not to

see the closure of many lines, although the branches to Old Meldrum (on 2 November 1931) and Boddam (on 31 October 1932) lost their passenger services. It was only after nationalisation that the GNoSR was effectively shrunk to the main line from Keith to Aberdeen alone.

The first postwar casualty came with the complete closure of the Boddam branch on 31 December 1948. This was followed on 2 February 1950 by the withdrawal of passenger services from the Alford branch (it closed completely on 7 November 1966) and on 1 October by the cessation of passenger services over the Macduff branch (it closed completely from Turriff to Macduff on 1 August 1961 and from Inveramsay to Turriff on 3 January 1966). For the bulk of the ex-GNoSR branches, the final death knell was to come with the Beeching Report; although efforts had been made to reduce operational costs — such as the use of railbuses on the line to Grantown on Spey (East) and the unique battery-powered multiple-unit on the Ballater branch — the economics of many of the ex-GNoSR lines were such that closures came rapidly during the mid-1960s. The branch to Lossiemouth succumbed on 6 April 1964; it was to close completely on 28 March 1966. The short Banff branch followed on 6 July 1964; it closed completely on 6 May 1968. This closure was followed on 3 May 1965 by withdrawal of passenger services from Maud to Peterhead (freight services were to follow on 7 September 1970) and on 4 October 1965 by withdrawal from Dyce to Fraserburgh. With the latter line, freight services were to survive until 6 October 1979. The line from Craigellachie to Boat of Garten succumbed on 18 October 1965 and was closed completely south of Aberlour on 4 November 1968. On 3 January 1966, the Old Meldrum branch was to close completely. On 28 February 1966 the Ballater line closed; freight services beyond Banchory ceased on 18 July of the same year and the rump of the branch, from Ferryhill to Banchory, closed completely in January 1967. The final passenger closures came on 6 May 1968 when the two routes from Keith and Grange to Elgin closed simultaneously. The coastal route was to close completely at the same time. The line beyond Dufftown to Elgin closed in stages between 1968 and 1971; the remaining section, from Keith to Dufftown, survived to serve a distillery and is now the target of a preservation scheme.

The past 50 years have not been kind to the lines inherited from the GNoSR; today, the national network comprises only the route from Aberdeen to Keith for passenger services, whilst freight continues to use the Waterloo route. The Dufftown line survives as a potential preserved line, but despite the huge investment in North Sea oil, based on Aberdeen, none of the other lines remains.

Now: 27 May 1998
The station layout here is still basically the same, but there has been a lot of new building around the station area, which has become extremely congested. The towers in the background were obscured by the steam from the 'D43' in the 'Then' photograph. Guild Street, from where most freight currently originates, is just to the right of the picture. *Author*

Aberdeen station (north end)

Then: 29 July 1953
Ex-Great Eastern Class B12/1 No 61502, one of 25 of this type of locomotive to be transferred to the GNoSR section in the 1930s, is pictured leaving the north end of the Joint station heading the 6.10pm service to Keith. These locomotives were nicknamed 'Hikers'. *Brian Morrison*

Now: 27 May 1998
Change has been dramatic at the north end of the station. Space in Aberdeen centre is at a premium and so a solution was found in building over the top of the station. This has resulted in a very drab and inhospitable environment; fortunately, however, the rest of the station is very much the opposite. The 'Then' photograph was taken a few yards further back than this picture, but the results would have been the same. In the background, Class 158 No 158720 is seen on a service to Inverness. *Author*

Cutler

Then: August 1965
A Cravens Class 105 DMU, heading towards Ballater, waits at the station of Cutler for a service towards Aberdeen to pass. The line from Aberdeen to Banchory via Cutler was opened on 8 September 1853 by the Deeside Railway. This station was located just under 7.5 miles from Aberdeen. *Andrew Muckley*

Aberdeen Harbour

Then: 22 May 1957
The four ex-GNoSR docks tanks, Classes X and Y, entered service in 1915 and were a regular sight around the docks for over 40 years. Under LNER ownership the quartet became Classes Z4 and Z5. This delightful picture shows 'Z5' 0-4-2T No 68192 as it crosses Market Street and heads into the main docks area. *J. Spencer Gilks*

Now: 27 May 1998
Sadly, the railways in the docks are now no more and the cobbled Market Street of 1957 has given way to a wide tarmacked road. The buildings on the right have survived, but to the left modernisation has taken place. The picture was taken from the pavement rather than the centre of the road — the speed and number of cars have increased dramatically over the years. *Author*

Now: 27 May 1998
The branch to Ballater, despite its royal connections (it served Balmoral Castle) and the introduction of diesel railbuses, was to lose its passenger services on 28 February 1966 and was to close completely on 2 January 1967. Today, one of the platforms survives, but everything else, with the exception of the bridge abutments, has disappeared. *Author*

Torphins

Then: Undated (pre-Grouping)
At 23.75 miles from Aberdeen, the station at Torphins was just over halfway to Ballater. This undated photograph shows a busy scene, with two trains passing; the Aberdeen-bound train would appear to be at least nine vehicles long, whilst the westbound service would appear to be headed by one of the GNoSR Class O 4-4-0s, of which nine were built by Kitson & Co in 1888. These locomotives were destined to become LNER Class D42 after Grouping. The line to Ballater opened as far as Banchory in 1853; the section from Banchory to Aboyne, via Torphins, opened on 2 December 1859. *Ian Allan Library*

Now: 26 May 1998
The Ballater branch lost its passenger services on 28 February 1966 and the section west of Culter was to close completely on 18 July 1966. The change here has been dramatic. Apart from the old railway bridge, from where I took this photograph of the new houses, everything to do with the railway has vanished. *Author*

Dinnet

Then: August 1965
This delightful picture shows a Cravens-built Class 105 DMU arriving from Ballater with a service for Aberdeen; a single passenger is ready to board the train. Dinnet station was situated 36.75 miles from Aberdeen and was on the section of line, from Aboyne to Ballater, which opened on 17 October 1866. *Andrew Muckley*

Now: 26 May 1998
Passenger services ceased over the Ballater branch on 28 February 1966 and freight was withdrawn on the following 18 July. As can be seen, nature has really taken hold here, but through the trees to the right is the station building, which is still in use, albeit today as an estate office. *Author*

Cambus o'May

Then: August 1965
The picturesque little halt at Cambus o'May was opened in 1876 and was situated some 3.5 miles from the terminus at Ballater.
Andrew Muckley

Now: 26 May 1998
The station lost its passenger services on 28 February 1966 and the line from Culter to Ballater was to close completely on 18 July 1966. Apart from the lack of track, nothing has changed very much over the past 33 years. As the notice proclaims, the station is now private property. Notice how the view of the River Dee at this point has now vanished due to the growth of the trees. *Author*

Ballater

Then: 14 July 1960
Ballater station was situated some 43.25 miles from Aberdeen. This picture shows the station area in 1960, at which time it looked immaculate; no doubt, it received special treatment as a result of the frequent visits by royalty on their way to Balmoral Castle. The section from Aboyne to Ballater opened on 17 October 1866. Pictured in the station ready to return with a service to Aberdeen is a two-car Gloucester-built DMU. It is worth mentioning that the experimental two-car battery multiple-unit, which is now preserved and based on the East Lancashire Railway, was introduced to the Deeside line in 1958. *Colin Boocock*

Now: 26 May 1998
Passenger services, despite royal patronage, were to cease on 28 February 1966 and freight succumbed on the following 18 July. The station and platform have been well preserved, as can be seen, and the yard area has been grassed over. The whole area is extremely neat and tidy. *Author*

Dyce

Then: 12 June 1959
This was the junction at which the Buchan line towards Ellon and Maud Junction headed north from the GNoSR main line towards Inverurie. The station is some 6.25 miles from Aberdeen and, as this photograph shows, was provided with a centre platform serving both lines as well as two outside platforms. This picture shows BR Standard Class 4MT No 80114 at the head of a train to Peterhead or Fraserburgh. The first station at Dyce opened on 12 September 1854 with the opening of the line from Kittybrewster to Huntly. The original station closed on 17 July 1861 when it was replaced by a new station, due south, with the opening of the line to Maud. *Author*

Now: 27 May 1998
Dyce station closed on 6 May 1968 but was to be reopened on 15 September 1984. The Buchan line platforms have now become a car park. The station is located close to Dyce (Aberdeen) Airport. Note the tall signalbox at the east end of the station; this is a feature of the station. Passenger services over the line to Maud ceased on 4 October 1965, although the line to Fraserburgh remained open for freight until 6 October 1979. *Author*

Maud Junction

Then: 12 June 1959
This was the point on the line north from Dyce where the lines to Peterhead and Fraserburgh divided. Since the line opened from Dyce to Mintlaw (on the Peterhead line) via Maud on 18 July 1861, the station has had several names; these include Brucklay, New Maud Junction and then Maud. The line from Maud to Fraserburgh opened on 24 April 1865. The line from Dyce to Peterhead and Fraserburgh was known as the Buchan Section. Here Standard Class 4MT No 80112 is pictured ready to leave for Fraserburgh. *Author*

Now (Fraserburgh side): 26 May 1998
The Fraserburgh line lost its passenger services on 4 October 1965 but freight was to survive until 4 October 1979. The station area has been beautifully restored and includes a small museum. The site forms part of the 54-mile long Formantine & Buchan Way. *Author*

Now (Peterhead side): 26 May 1998
Passenger services between Maud and Peterhead were withdrawn slightly before those to Fraserburgh, on 3 May 1965, and freight was to cease over this section on 7 September 1970. As with the Fraserburgh side of the station, the Peterhead platforms have also been well restored. *Author*

Fraserburgh Junction

Then: 12 June 1959
The St Coombs branch headed east away from the Fraserburgh-Maud Junction line just south of Fraserburgh. Here Standard Class 4MT No 80111 sets off south with the 9.46am fish train to Aberdeen (and eventually London), whilst the St Coombs branch can be seen heading off into the sand dunes. The St Coombs branch, the last section of the GNoSR to be constructed, was opened on 1 July 1903. *Author*

Now: 26 May 1998
The St Coombs branch lost its passenger services on 3 May 1965 and was to close completely at the same time. Passenger services to Fraserburgh were withdrawn on 4 October 1965, with freight surviving until 4 October 1979. The overbridge from where the 'Then' photograph was taken has long since disappeared and the road has been straightened out. The track alignment can, however, still be picked out in the centre of the picture. *Author*

Cairnbulg

Then: 12 June 1959
The main intermediate station on the line to St Coombs — there were also two halts — was at Cairnbulg, 3.6 miles from Fraserburgh. The local branch engine at the time, Standard Class 2MT No 78045, is pictured departing with a service for Fraserburgh. *Author*

Fraserburgh

Then: 12 June 1959
The lines to Fraserburgh and Peterhead split at Maud Junction, 31.25 miles from Aberdeen, after leaving the main line at Dyce, six miles west of the Granite City. The station at Fraserburgh was opened on 24 April 1865 by the Formantine & Buchan Railway. Fraserburgh was always a busy fishing port and, as can be seen in the picture, there were usually plenty of fish vans in the yard. Standard Class 4MT No 80114, a class which monopolised the services at the end of steam, is pictured leaving with the 9.17am service to Aberdeen. It will join with the portion from Peterhead at Maud. The small engine shed was just to the left of the picture. *Author*

Now: 26 May 1998
Passenger services to Fraserburgh ceased on 4 October 1965 and freight on 4 October 1979. The railway land has been completely redeveloped into an industrial estate and there is now little to indicate that a railway ever existed in the town. Fraserburgh today appears to be a busy place which could have made good use of the railway had it survived. *Author*

Now: 26 May 1998
The line between St Coombs and Fraserburgh closed completely on 3 May 1965. Today, the station site at Cairnbulg has been landscaped although it is still possible to determine the location of the level crossing and many of the surrounding buildings are largely unchanged. *Author*

St Coombs

Then: 12 June 1959
The 5.125-mile long Light Railway from Fraserburgh to St Coombs ran mainly through the sand dunes and a golf course along the seafront of Fraserburgh Bay. The line opened on 1 July 1903, being the last extension opened by the GNoSR. Standard Class 2MT No 78045, which went new to Scotland, finished up as the branch engine and is pictured ready to leave for Fraserburgh. The branch was worked for a time by ex-Great Eastern Class F4 2-4-2Ts, which were fitted with cow catchers front and rear for this duty; apparently, the reason for the cow catchers had been eliminated by the time that No 78045 was working the line. Ivatt 2-6-0s Nos 46460 and 46461 were also regular performers over the line. Note the gentleman cutting the grass; not something that is seen these days on the railways. *Author*

Now: 26 May 1998
The St Coombs line closed completely on 3 May 1965 and, as can be seen, the whole station area has been redeveloped with housing. As a result, there is now no trace of the fact that the town was once served by a railway. *Author*

Alford

Then: 7 July 1961
Alford was the terminus of the 16-mile branch which left the main Aberdeen-Huntly route at Kintore, 13.25 miles from Aberdeen. The line opened on 25 March 1859. By the date of the Then photograph, passenger services had already been withdrawn — on 2 January 1950 — but freight remained. Here the daily freight is being shunted; the motive power is either an Ivatt Class 2MT or a BR Standard 2-6-0. *Ian Allan Library*

Peterhead

Then: 12 June 1959
The station at Peterhead was 38 miles from Dyce. It was opened on 3 July 1862 when the line from Mintlaw was extended to the town. The station was very busy, particularly with fish traffic, as can be seen in this photograph of Standard Class 4MT No 80029 leaving with a two-coach train. Following the demise of steam in the area, services to Peterhead were worked by a mixture of Cravens-built DMUs, North British Type 2s and BRCW Type 2s. The station was also provided with a small two-road engine shed. *Author*

Now: 26 May 1998
Today, all traces of the railway at Peterhead have been obliterated with a new academy and community centre built on the site. Passenger services to Peterhead ceased on 3 May 1965 with freight following on 7 September 1970. *Author*

Now: 26 May 1998
This part of the old goods yard has been redeveloped, but the station and immediate area have been well restored by the Alford Valley Railway, where there is a museum and track, situated to the right of this view. The Alford Valley Railway operates a 2ft-gauge line for some 3km. Adjacent to the site at Alford is the Grampian Transport Museum. *Author*

Inverurie

Then: Undated (pre-Grouping)

The first station opened here on 1 May 1866, but this was replaced by a new station, just to the north, which was opened on 10 February 1902. The construction of the new station was probably the result of the transfer of the GNoSR's main works from Kittybrewster; the original works had by the start of the 20th century proved inadequate and a new facility was constructed at Inverurie, the last of which was completed in 1905. As a result, Inverurie grew to become one of the most important locations on the GNoSR. The picture is undated, but shows one of the three GNoSR Class C 4-4-0s (later LNER Class D39) which were built by Neilson & Co in 1879 and withdrawn in 1926/27. Inverurie Works finally closed in 1969; for the last few years of its life, the works was mainly involved in the scrapping of redundant steam locomotives. *Ian Allan Library*

Now: 26 May 1998

The ex-GNoSR main line continues to operate and the station at Inverurie, situated 16.75 miles from Aberdeen, is still open. It is, however, much reduced in status. The bay platforms have gone as have most of the buildings. A small amount of freight uses the sidings at the west end. *Author*

Macduff

Then: 16 June 1949

Macduff was the terminus of the 29.75-mile long branch which left the ex-GNoSR main line at Inveramsay, 20.5 miles from Aberdeen. The railway arrived here on 1 July 1872 when the line was extended from Gerrymill; the line had opened from Inveramsay to Gerrymill in two stages, on 5 September 1857 when the line was opened from Inveramsay to Turriff and on 4 June 1860 when it was extended from Turriff to Gerrymill. Macduff and Banff are only about one mile apart, separated by the River Deveron, which flows into Banff Bay. This photograph shows the length of the yard and the station very well. An ex-GNoSR 4-4-0 appears to be ready to leave with a train, whilst careful examination of the bottom left of the picture shows the now preserved Class D40 *Gordon Highlander*, then No 62277, half inside the small shed. *H. C. Casserley*

Now: 24 May 1998

Passenger services over the line to Macduff ceased on 1 October 1951, two years after the date of the 'Then' photograph. Freight continued over the whole route until 1 August 1961 when the section north of Turriff was closed completely. The line from Turriff to Inveramsay was to close completely on 3 January 1966. Today, all signs of the railway have gone, with the exception of the shed which is still standing and is visible at the bottom left of the photograph. The area is now used as a boat repair yard. *Author*

Cairnie Junction

Then: 10 May 1968

This was the point where the two routes to Elgin went their separate ways: one via Keith and the inland route and the other via the north route and the coast. There was a triangular junction to the west of the station. The main line from Huntly to Keith opened on 10 October 1856 and the line north towards Portsoy followed on 30 July 1859. The third side of the triangle, Grange South to Grange North, opened on 1 May 1886. The station here opened as 'Cairnie

Platform' in 1897, becoming 'Cairnie Junction' in June 1919. The station, which is 48.25 miles from Aberdeen, was provided with an island platform. One of the Class 120 InterCity DMUs is pictured passing *en route* to Elgin. The station, and the line northwards, had closed four days earlier, on 6 May 1968. The line towards Tillynaught can be seen branching off to the right in the distance.
C. W. R. Bowman

Now: 24 May 1998

As noted already, the line towards Tillynaught lost its passenger services on 6 May 1968 and was closed completely at the same time. As can be seen, the changes here have been dramatic, with both the junction and the station obliterated. Today only the single-track main line between Inverness and Aberdeen bisects the site.
Author

Tillynaught

Then: 12 June 1959

This was a very imposing station considering that it was in such a remote area. The line between Cairnie and Portsoy, via Tillynaught, was opened by the Banff, Portsoy & Strathisla Railway on 30 July 1859, at which time the six-mile branch between Tillynaught and Banff, which headed east from here, was also opened. The main line continued towards the coast and onwards to Elgin some 29 miles away. Standard 2-6-4T No 80121 has arrived from Cairnie Junction and is pictured ready to leave for Elgin, having made a connection with the Banff train, which can be seen just to the left of the station building, being worked on this occasion by Standard Class 2MT No 78053. *Author*

Now: 24 May 1998

The branch to Banff lost its passenger services on 6 July 1964 and was to close completely on 6 May 1968 at which time the line between Cairnie Junction and Portsoy and thence to Elgin was also to lose both its passenger services and close completely. Today, all signs of the railway have gone from this location with the exception of a narrow road to the site which is still called 'Station Road'. *Author*

Banff

Then: 5 July 1963

The station nestled under the cliff, virtually on the seafront, and was opened as 'Banff Harbour' on 30 July 1859 by the Banff, Portsoy & Strathisla Railway. The station was renamed 'Banff' by the LNER in 1928. The branch was being operated when recorded here by BR Standard Class 2MT No 78045. This locomotive went new to the GNoSR section in October 1955 and was to be withdrawn in January 1966. The now preserved ex-GNoSR 4-4-0 *Gordon Highlander* worked the branch prior to its withdrawal. The platform at Banff was so arranged that there was no space for a run-round loop, with the result that trains had to be reversed out of the station to facilitate the run round. *W. G. Sumner*

Now: 24 May 1998

The branch from Tillynaught to Banff lost its passenger services in July 1964 and was to close completely on 6 May 1968. Today, nothing remains of the branch terminus and the road has been realigned to take advantage of the former railway site. *Author*

Lossiemouth

Then: Undated
This is an undated view of Lossiemouth station, which was the terminus of a branch which ran for 5.5 miles due north from Elgin. The line continued beyond the passenger station to serve the harbour. The line opened from Elgin to Lossiemouth on 10 August 1852. The locomotive illustrated is one of the three Great North of Scotland Class G 4-4-0s; these were later classified 'D48' by the LNER. The last of the class was withdrawn in November 1934, which gives some indication as to the antiquity of this view. *Ian Allan Library*

Now: 24 May 1998
Passenger services between Elgin and Lossiemouth ceased on 6 April 1964 and freight services succumbed on 28 March 1966. The whole area has been converted into a car park. I was interested to note that further on, by the harbour, the rails of the line could still be seen embedded into the roadway. *Author*

Portknockie

Then: 4 August 1962

The railway did not arrive at this point until relatively late. The line between Garmouth and Tochieneal via Portknockie and Cullen opened on 5 April 1886; this route completed the GNoSR's coast line from Elgin to Keith via Portessie. The line from Portsoy to Tochieneal opened on 1 April 1884, to be followed on 12 April 1884 by that between Elgin and Garmouth and on 1 August 1884 by the line between Keith and Portsoy. This two-car DMU, headed by Cravens-built No 51475 (later designated Class 105) forms the 11.50am service from Elgin to Keith. Note that the single-line token is being passed to the driver. *A. A. Vickers*

Now: 24 May 1998

Passenger services over the line were withdrawn on 6 May 1968, at which time the line was to close completely. This was a difficult location to sort out, as the little road bridge had gone and the whole area had been levelled. To the back of me are new houses and it appeared that this site was also soon to be redeveloped. The sea is now visible at the top right of the photograph. *Author*

Elgin

Then: 1952
This is a view of the ex-GNoSR station which served Elgin. The station opened on 10 August 1852 with the line to Lossiemouth. Six years later, on 25 March 1858, the Highland Railway reached Elgin, with the opening of the line from Forres; it was extended eastwards to Keith on 18 August 1858. The GNoSR presence in Elgin was enhanced on 30 December 1861 with the opening of the line towards Rothes and on 12 April 1884 by the opening of the line to Garmouth. There was also a link to the HR station. This photograph shows one of Keith's two Standard Class 4MT 2-6-4Ts, No 80122, ready to depart with the 9.30am service to Aberdeen via Craigellachie. *J. C. W. Halliday*

Now: 26 May 1998
Today the ex-GNoSR station is closed and all passenger services at Elgin are concentrated on the ex-HR station with trains operating only over the main line between Forres and Keith. Passenger services to Lossiemouth ceased on 6 April 1964 with the line closing completely on 28 March 1966. The lines to Garmouth and Rothes saw their last passenger services on 6 May 1968; the former was to close completely at the same time whilst freight services continued to operate over the line to Rothes until 4 November 1968. Today the main station building is in use as offices and is still intact, but all the platforms and track have been cleared. Elsewhere, the goods yard is still open and sees use virtually daily. *Author*

Keith Junction

Then: 11 June 1959

The GNoSR arrived here first, with the opening of the line from Huntly on 10 October 1856. The town became an important centre for the GNoSR with a locomotive shed being built and another station, Keith Town (originally called 'Earlsmill'), three-quarters of a mile closer to the centre and situated on the line towards Dufftown, which opened on 21 February 1862. The Highland Railway (originally as the Inverness & Aberdeen Junction Railway) arrived on 18 August 1858,

making an end-on connection with the GNoSR and thereby permitting through trains between Inverness and Aberdeen. There was great hostility between the two companies in general and particularly in Keith. After the opening of the Aviemore to Forres line, Keith became less important to the HR and it transferred most of its locomotives to Forres. In this view we see a local Class K2 2-6-0, No 61741, ready to leave for Forres with a westbound train. *Author*

Now: 24 May 1998

The station is well used today and, as can be seen, this part of the station has altered very little, although a new booking area has been provided together with a car park. On the other hand, the station is still signalled by semaphores. Keith Town station lost its passenger services on 6 May 1968, although the line to Dufftown survived for freight for a further 20 years and was also used for special trains until the early 1990s; today, the Keith-Dufftown line is the subject of a preservation scheme. *Author*

Dufftown

Then: June 1971
The GNoSR arrived here first on 21 February 1862 with the opening of the line from Keith; the line was extended southwards from Dufftown to Craigellachie on 1 July 1863. By the date of this photograph, the line from Keith to Elgin had already lost its passenger services — on 6 May 1968. Freight, however, was still being run over the line as far south as Aberlour. *Andrew Muckley*

Now: 24 May 1998
The line south of Dufftown as far as Aberlour closed completely shortly after the date of the 'Then' photograph, on 15 November 1971. The line remained open as far as Dufftown for freight traffic to a distillery; this traffic survived until the late 1980s. Thereafter, the line to Dufftown was to remain in operation solely for the use of special passenger services until complete closure from 1 April 1991. The site of the station became derelict after closure, but the Keith & Dufftown Preservation Society has been formed with a view to restoring the line. The project is still in its very early stages, but as can be seen considerable work has been undertaken on the station and platform, whilst the yard contains various items of rolling stock. The main item of stock comprises the Class 140 DMU prototype cars, Nos 55500/55501, which were built at Derby in 1981. It would be a splendid line to reopen and one wishes the society well. *Author*

Craigellachie

Then: 1950s

This was once an important junction of the GNoSR, with lines radiating to Boat of Garten, Elgin and Keith. It was on 1 July 1863 that Craigellachie was linked to Dufftown (on the line to Keith), Aberlour (on the line to Boat of Garten) and Dandaleith (on the line to Elgin). It was originally known as 'Craigellachie Junction' when it opened, but became simple 'Craigellachie' in 1904. This delightful picture, which is full of railway interest, shows Class B1 4-6-0 No 61346 arriving with the 2pm service from Elgin to Aberdeen. *J. C. W. Halliday*

Now: 24 May 1998

Passenger services over the line from Craigellachie to Boat of Garten ceased on 18 October 1965 and those from Keith to Elgin followed on 6 May 1968. The line from Craigellachie to Elgin closed completely on 4 November 1968. Freight services continued to operate through Craigellachie until the line between Dufftown and Aberlour was closed completely on 15 November 1971. Today, the westbound platform survives, but the rest of the area has been redeveloped into a car park and cycle/walkway. Little else remains to remind visitors that this was once a significant railway location. *Author*

Rothes

Then: August 1965
Rothes is 9.75 miles from Elgin on the inland route from Cairnie Junction via Craigellachie. The railway first reached Rothes via a link to Orton, on the main line between Elgin and Keith, which opened on 23 August 1858; the line was extended to Dandaleith, towards Craigellachie, on 23 December 1858. The line was extended north from Rothes to Elgin on 30 December 1861 and five years later, in 1866, the original line between Rothes and Orton was to close completely. Here one of the five Park Royal railbuses, all of which finished their days in Scotland, is shown calling with a service to Elgin. *Andrew Muckley*

Now: 24 May 1998
Passenger services between Craigellachie and Elgin ceased on 6 May 1968 and the line was to close completely on 4 November 1968. Virtually nothing remains of the station. The site is now used as a car park, although the trackbed from the level crossing is in use as a pathway across a small bridge over the local stream. *Author*

Longmorn

Then: August 1965
Three miles out of Elgin on the line to Craigellachie is Longmorn, which served the small village and local distillery. The line between Rothes and Elgin opened on 30 December 1861. This lovely station scene shows the Elgin-Craigellachie railbus calling. This is another view of one of the five Park Royal railbuses which finished their operational careers in Scotland. *Author*

Now: 26 May 1998
Passenger services between Elgin and Craigellachie were withdrawn on 6 May 1968. The line was to close completely on the following 4 November. The station and platforms are still intact; in fact the station building is in very good condition. It would appear that the railway land has been acquired by the local distillery. *Author*

Carron

Then: August 1965
This station is the next one south from Aberlour on the line towards Boat of Garten. It is on the section of line which opened to services on 11 July 1863. Here we see one of the Park Royal railbuses, en route from Aviemore to Elgin. *Andrew Muckley*

Aberlour

Then: August 1965
This was the first station south of Craigellachie on the line towards Boat of Garten. The line opened from Craigellachie to Aberlour on 1 July 1863 and extended from Aberlour to Abernethy on 11 July 1863. Here another of the quintet of AC-built railbuses calls at the station.
Andrew Muckley

Now: 24 May 1998
Passenger services ceased between Craigellachie and Boat of Garten on 18 October 1965, shortly after the date of the 'Then' photograph. The line was closed completely south of Aberlour on 4 November 1968. The section of line between Aberlour and Dufftown remained operational until 15 November 1971. As can be seen, the station, platform and nameboard still stand and are in very good condition and are well maintained, with a very pleasant grassed area over the former trackbed. The station appeared to be used as a local community centre and, when I called on a Sunday morning, local ladies were serving teas and coffees to raise funds for charity. *Author*

Now: 24 May 1998
As can be seen, the station area has altered dramatically. The station building and platform still stand to the right of the picture, but the area has been very nicely landscaped and now appears to be part of the site occupied by Ballantines Imperial Distillery (established in 1897). No doubt, this distillery once despatched and received goods by rail. Passenger services through Carron ceased on 18 October 1965 with freight being withdrawn on 4 November 1968. *Author*

Grantown on Spey East

Then: August 1965
This station was situated 24 miles south of Craigellachie. The GNoSR line from Boat of Garten, where a junction was made with the Highland Railway line from Aviemore to Forres, to Abernethy (Nethy Bridge) opened on 11 July 1863. The station was known as 'Grantown' until 5 June 1950 when it was retitled 'Grantown on Spey'. The 'East' suffix was to differentiate the station from 'West', which served the ex-HR line. *Andrew Muckley*

Now: 24 May 1998
As can be seen, the station and land are derelict with no development having taken place in the 30 years since the line closed. The station seems to have stood up well to the elements over the years. The line between Boat of Garten and Craigellachie lost its passenger services on 18 October 1965 and the section between Boat of Garten and Aberlour was to close completely on 4 November 1968. *Author*

Nethy Bridge

Then: 1896
The line from Aberlour to Abernethy, the last GNoSR station on the route towards Boat of Garten, opened on 1 July 1863 and the final section, from Abernethy to Boat of Garten (a distance of 4.75 miles), followed on 1 August 1866. The station changed its name from Abernethy to Nethy Bridge on 1 November 1867. This very early photograph shows one of the nine 2-4-0s designed by Cowan and built by Robert Stephenson & Co. The last of the class was withdrawn in 1909. *Ian Allan Library*

Now: 24 May 1998
The station house and platform still survive; the former is now a private residence. The track and yard area are undeveloped. The line lost its passenger services on 18 October 1965 and freight ceased on 4 November 1968. As can be seen in the inset photograph, 33 years after closure, the station nameboard was still standing. *Author (2)*

Highland Railway

The Highland Railway, based at Inverness, was one of the three Scottish companies which passed to LMS in 1923. Its network of lines, running north, south, east and west from Inverness, was perhaps the most sparsely populated of any of the pre-Grouping railways, with the possible exception of the neighbouring Great North of Scotland, and yet, more than 75 years since the Grouping, many of the lines inherited from the HR continue to provide an essential service to the communities of the region. Despite threats to the remaining lines, most recently in the Serpell Report, the lines from Perth to Inverness and from Inverness towards Aberdeen and to Kyle of Lochalsh, Thurso and Wick remain.

The first section of the future Highland Railway opened, under the auspices of the Inverness & Nairn Railway, between Inverness and Nairn on 5 November 1855. The line was extended eastwards to Forres on 22 December 1857 and then to Elgin on 25 March 1858. The link to Keith, and thus a connection with the GNoSR line towards Aberdeen, opened on 18 August 1858. The first section of the main line north from Perth, from Stanley Junction to Dunkeld opened on 7 April 1856. The line was extended from Dunkeld to Pitlochry on 1 June 1863 and to Aviemore on 9 September 1863. The

final link in the chain of railways from Perth to Inverness at this stage came with the opening of the Aviemore to Forres line on 3 August 1863.

By this date, work was also in progress on the line to the far north. The line from Inverness to Dingwall opened on 11 June 1862. It was extended to Invergordon on 25 May 1863. Further extensions saw the line extended to Meikle Ferry on 1 June 1864, to Bonar Bridge

Ballinluig Junction (main line)

Then: 13 June 1959
Ballinluig was the junction for the branch to Aberfeldy, which headed west off the Highland main line and across the River Tummel. The station opened on 1 June 1863 under the auspices of the Inverness & Perth Junction Railway along with the line from Dunkeld to Pitlochry. Here an up freight, headed by Inverness-allocated Class 5 No 45192, waits for a northbound train to pass before entering the single line section to Dunkeld. The rear of the branch line train can be seen on the left. *Author*

on 1 October 1864, to Golspie on 13 April 1868, to Helmsdale on 19 June 1871 and to Wick and Thurso (via Georgemas Junction — the most northerly in Britain) on 28 July 1874. The opening of the line to Kyle of Lochalsh commenced with the section from Dingwall to Strome Ferry on 19 August 1870; it was extended through to the terminus at Kyle of Lochalsh on 2 November 1897.

In terms of HR main lines, the final development came with the opening of the new route from Aviemore to Inverness which significantly reduced the mileage on the line between Perth and Inverness. This route was opened in three stages: from Aviemore to Carrbridge on 6 July 1892, from Carrbridge to Daviot on 8 July and thence to Inverness on 1 November 1898. With the completion of this route, the importance of the original main line via Boat of Garten was much reduced.

Apart from the main lines, the HR also constructed a number of branches. The line from Alves to Burghead opened on 22 November 1862; it was extended to Hopeman on 10 October 1892. The line to Aberfeldy, from Ballinluig, opened on 3 July 1865. The Strathpeffer branch, from Fodderty Junction, opened on 3 June 1885. Five branches opened relatively late: Fochabers (on 23 October 1893); Fortrose (1 February 1894); Fort George (1 July 1899); Dornoch (2 June 1902); and Lybster (on 1 July 1903).

The Grouping years saw the ex-HR network shrink slightly, with the loss of passenger services on the lines to Hopeman and Fochabers — both succumbing on 14 September 1931 — whilst passenger

services also ceased on the short Fort George branch on 5 April 1943. The only ex-HR line to close completely during this period was the line between Wick and Lybster, on 3 April 1944. The Strathpeffer branch lost its passenger services on 23 April 1946.

With the exception of the Lybster line, the entire HR network passed to BR at Nationalisation. However, it was not long before further economies occurred. The short Strathpeffer branch closed completely on 26 March 1951. This was followed by the complete closure of the section of line between Burghead and Hopeman on 30 December 1957; the line from Alves to Burghead remains operational for freight today. The Fort George line was to close completely on 11 August 1958 followed by that to Fortrose — which had lost its passenger services on 1 October 1951 — on 13 June 1960. The same day was to witness the withdrawal of passenger services over, and complete closure of, the branch from Dornoch to The Mound; in this line's latter existence, it had been operated by ex-GWR 0-6-0PTs, which had been sent north for these duties. The Aberfeldy branch was to lose its passenger services and close completely on 3 May 1965. The final section of the ex-HR which has disappeared since Nationalisation, the line from Forres to Aviemore — the old main line — lost its passenger services on 18 October 1965 at which stage it closed completely north of Boat of Garten. The southern section, from Aviemore to Boat of Garten, closed completely on 4 November 1968.

Today, much of the erstwhile Highland Railway forms part of the national network — with trains running over the Perth-Inverness main line, over the route to Elgin and over the lines to Kyle of Lochalsh, Thurso and Wick. Part of the old main line, from Aviemore to Boat of Garten, is preserved by the Strathspey Railway; the preservation company started to operate into Aviemore station proper during 1998 and the railway is currently making good progress with its long-term aim of reconstructing the line north of Boat of Garten to Grantown on Spey (West).

Now: 21 May 1998
The station at Ballinluig closed on 3 May 1965 along with the branch to Aberfeldy. All signs of the station and junction have gone and passengers passing on this fast section of the Highland main line will be unaware that the station ever existed. *Author*

Ballinluig Junction (branch)

Then: 16 June 1959
The train to Aberfeldy waits for the connection from Perth at the branch platform. Ex-CR McIntosh Class 439 0-4-4T No 55218 was sub-shedded at Aberfeldy at this time from its home shed at Perth. A Class 5MT can just be seen on the main line waiting for a northbound train to arrive to clear the single line section from Dunkeld. The Aberfeldy branch opened on 3 July 1865. *Author*

Now: 21 May 1998
As with the previous 'Now' photograph showing the main line scene at Ballinluig, all traces of the station, with the exception of part of the platform edge deep in the undergrowth, have vanished. Even the bridge across the river has gone; its site appeared to be part of the new road layout. The Aberfeldy branch lost its passenger services on 3 May 1965 at which time the line was closed completely. *Author*

Aberfeldy

Then: 13 June 1959
This was the terminus of the 8.75-mile branch from Ballinluig. It was opened on 3 July 1865 by the Inverness & Perth Junction Railway, later becoming part of the Highland Railway. In the last days of steam on the line, one of the ex-CR McIntosh Class 439 0-4-4Ts was the usual motive power; the locomotive was allocated to Perth but sub-shedded at Aberfeldy. On this occasion No 55218 was working the branch and is pictured waiting to depart with a service to Ballinluig. *Author*

Grandtully

Then: 1962
This station was the only intermediate station on the Aberfeldy branch and was located almost halfway between the junction and terminus. It was opened on 3 July 1865. This delightful picture shows Birmingham RCW Type 2 (later Class 26) No D5336 (later No 26036) arriving with the 10.46am train from Ballinluig. *W. A. C. Smith*

Now: 21 May 1998
Passenger services over the branch ceased on 3 May 1965. As a result the line failed by just two months to see its centenary. Freight had ceased four months earlier, on 25 January 1965. Evidence of the platform edge can be seen through the trees at the site, which has become a car park and picnic area since closure. *Author*

Now: 21 May 1998
As can be seen, all traces of the railway station and area in the town have now disappeared. The area has been reused as a car park. Freight services between Ballinluig and Aberfeldy ceased on 25 January 1965 with passenger services succumbing on 3 May 1965. *Author*

Pitlochry

Then: 22 August 1960
This very pleasant station serves the delightful town of Pitlochry. The main line opened from Dunkeld, in the south, to Pitlochry on 1 June 1863 and, on the following 9 September, the route was extended from Pitlochry northwards to Aviemore. Here Pickersgill Class 72 4-4-0 No 54486 is caught shunting some wagons into the yard and what was probably a Blair Atholl-Perth pick-up freight. Blair Atholl normally had one or two members of the class sub-shedded from Perth. *S. Summerson*

Now: 21 May 1998
The station remains today, serving trains between Perth and Inverness, and in 1998 was looking in better shape than it did in 1960. The footbridge, in particular, stood out well in its black and white paint scheme. Superpower for the 13.30 Inverness-Mossend freight (6D46) is provided in the form of two Res-liveried Class 47/4s, Nos 47572 *Ely Cathedral* and 47501 *Craftsman*, although only the former was actually working. *Author*

Blair Atholl

Then: 13 June 1959

This station is situated 35.25 miles from Perth and is the point where the 18-mile climb to the summit at Druimuachdar begins; this is the highest railway summit in the British Isles at 1,484ft. Standard Class 4MT No 80126, which at this time was the only representative of the class allocated to Perth, is pictured arriving with a local train from Perth; the locomotive will run-round the train before heading south again. A small sub-shed was located at Blair Atholl to service the station pilot and banking locomotives in steam days. The line through Blair Atholl, from Pitlochry to Aviemore, opened on 9 September 1863. *Author*

Now: 21 May 1998

The 14.35 service from Inverness to Edinburgh is pictured in the platform, having arrived a few minutes earlier; the train is formed of Class 158 No 158727. Freight facilities were withdrawn from the station on 7 November 1966, but I noticed that the sidings to the left had recently been cleared out; this was possibly for the loading of timber traffic. *Author*

Dalnaspidal

Then: 10 June 1957
This station is situated about two miles south of the summit at Druimuachdar (1,484ft) and is on the section of the Highland main line which opened on 9 September 1863. It is a remote location with little housing in the area. Here ex-CR McIntosh Class 812 0-6-0 No 57586, allocated to Aviemore, was on permanent way duties. *Author*

Now: 21 May 1998
The station at Dalnaspidal closed on 3 May 1965. As can be seen, the signalbox on the down platform is still in existence, but there is little otherwise for the passengers to see from the passing Class 158 units which now monopolise the passenger services over the line, except for the Euston-Inverness sleepers. The main A9 trunk road passes within about 100yd. *Author*

Newtonmore

Then: 1923

This location is about 68 miles south of Inverness and about one mile up the gradient towards Druimuachdar Summit from the north. The summit is situated about 16 miles to the south. This picture shows one of the Highland Railway 'Small Ben' class 4-4-0s, No 8 *Ben Clebrig*. The locomotive was built in 1899 and was withdrawn in 1939. This important station on the Highland main line opened, along with the Pitlochry-Aviemore section, on 9 September 1863. *Ian Allan Library (20189)*

Now: 22 May 1998

This wide-angle view is used in order to show more of the old station building and to illustrate the fact that the line has been singled through Newtonmore, although the old up platform still exists. The station building is now in private hands. *Author*

Aviemore

Then:

This photograph is undated but must be prior to 1935 as that was the year in which LMS No 14688 *Thurso Castle* was withdrawn from service. No 14688 had been built by the North British Locomotive Co in 1913. The train is pictured entering Aviemore station from the south, with the station nameboard recording the location as 'Aviemore Junction'. The first railway to reach Aviemore was the line from Boat of Garten, which opened on 3 August 1863. The line was extended southwards to Pitlochry on 9 September 1863. Aviemore became a junction with the opening of the line north to Carrbridge (and later Inverness) on 6 July 1892.
H. C. Casserley

Now: 22 May 1998

On a dismal morning, the 07.10 from Glasgow to Inverness arrives at 09.52 formed of Class 158 No 158730. I have included a view looking north (bottom left), rather than a direct comparison shot, to illustrate how the station has been refurbished in 1998. Work included the installation of a fence to separate services over the Highland main line from those of the preserved Strathspey Railway; the latter was due to start running scheduled services into Aviemore shortly after this photograph was taken. The original HR main line to Boat of Garten was closed to passenger services on 18 October 1965 and to freight on 4 November 1968. The section from just north of Aviemore station to Boat of Garten reopened as the Strathspey Railway in 1978.
Author

Carrbridge

Then: Undated (c1950)

The railway bridge crossing the River Dalnain at Carrbridge is about half a mile north of the station and is located only a few yards away from the main A9 road. Here a couple of ex-CR Pickersgill 4-4-0s, Nos 54488 and 54463, are pictured returning to Aviemore after assisting northbound trains to Slochd Summit, 5.5 miles north of this location. The gradient to Slochd was mainly at 1 in 60/70 and several locomotives of this type worked out their final years piloting trains over the summits at Slochd and Druimuachdar. The line north from Carrbridge to Daviot opened on 8 July 1897. *L. H. Buchanan*

Now: 22 May 1998

I had guessed correctly that a two-car Class 158 would fit nicely on to the bridge; however, I had not guessed that the 10.30 from Inverness to Edinburgh would be formed of a four-car train. The unit illustrated is No 158746. *Author*

Carrbridge station

Then: August 1965
It was in 1983 that British Rail changed the name of the station from the original 'Carr Bridge' to 'Carrbridge'. The station opened on 6 July 1892 when the line north from Aviemore was completed. The section north from Carrbridge to Daviot was to open on 8 July 1897; the final section in the HR's new main line from Aviemore to Inverness, from Daviot to Inverness, was to open on 1 November 1898. This photograph shows the station looking north. *Andrew Muckley*

Now: 22 May 1998
There are 33 years between the dates of these two photographs and, as can be seen, little has changed at the station. The signals have gone and new lighting has been installed, whilst goods facilities were withdrawn in February 1967. The station building is now used by Railtrack rather than passengers, but the footbridge and buildings remain in good condition. *Author*

Boat of Garten

Then: 1937
The station nameboard shows 'Boat of Garten, change here for the London & North Eastern Railway and Tomintoul'. The ex-GNoSR line from Craigellachie formed a junction with the ex-HR line from Aviemore to Forres at Boat of Garten. The line from Forres to Aviemore opened on 3 August 1863 under the auspices of the Inverness & Perth Junction Railway. The GNoSR route followed on 1 August 1866 with the opening of the line from Abernethy (Nethy Bridge). *Ian Allan Library (7388)*

Slochd

Then: Undated (c1950)
This interesting photograph shows a Stanier Class 5MT approaching at the head of an up passenger train, whilst an ex-CR 4-4-0 waits to detach from a 'down' freight train and return to Aviemore. The line north from Carrbridge to Daviot opened on 8 July 1897. *L. H. Buchanan*

Now: 22 May 1998
Over the past half century, not a great deal has changed at this location, although the signals have been replaced. The major change has occurred in the background, where the A9 has been improved. The old road still exists as a lay-by and is today a good location to observe the trains operating over the line whilst an almost constant stream of lorries and cars pass on the main road. *Author*

Now: 24 May 1998
The Strathspey Railway reopened the line from Aviemore to Boat of Garten and has restored the station into the fine condition we see in this photograph. Currently, the Strathspey Railway is in process of extending its line northwards to Broomhill (about four miles away) with the ultimate intention of reopening the line to Grantown on Spey West. The ex-GNoSR route lost its passenger services on 18 October 1965 and was to close completely on 4 November 1968. The ex-HR line from Aviemore to Forres was also to lose its passenger services on 18 October 1965, at which time the section north of Boat of Garten was to close completely. The section between Aviemore and Boat of Garten was to lose its freight services on 4 November 1968. *Author*

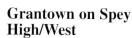

Grantown on Spey High/West

Then: 23 June 1967
This small town was provided with two stations: East was served by trains over the ex-GNoSR line and West by those on the ex-HR line from Aviemore to Forres. The Highland line was opened on 3 August 1863 at which time the station was known as 'Grantown High'. It became 'Grantown on Spey High' on 1 June 1912 and 'Grantown on Spey West' on 5 June 1950. By the date of this photograph, passenger services between Aviemore and Forres had already been withdrawn — on 18 October 1965 — and the line north of Boat of Garten closed completely. The view recorded here shows the line in a moribund state awaiting track lifting. *J. M. Boyes*

Now: 24 May 1998
On my visit there was little to remind me that the railway had once existed at this point, although the station building was still occupied behind the line of trees on the left of the photograph. The southern section of the line, from Aviemore to Boat of Garten, has been reopened by the Strathspey Railway which is currently restoring the line to Broomhill, with the intention of eventually reopening as far as Grantown on Spey. *Author*

Kinloss

Then: 28 June 1966
A cross-country (later Class 120) three-car Swindon-built DMU leaves Kinloss on the 11.45am Aberdeen-Inverness 3hr express. The first station to serve Kinloss opened with the short-lived line to Findhorn; this line opened on 16 April 1860 but lost its passenger services as long ago as 1 January 1869 and was to close completely in 1880. Despite efforts to reopen the line, the Findhorn branch was destined never to reopen with the result that the station at Kinloss was relocated to serve the Forres-Elgin line. The main line through Kinloss had opened earlier, on 25 March 1858. The station was located some 28 miles from Inverness. *J. M. Boyes*

Forres

Then: 15 June 1956
The first station opened in Forres on 25 March 1858 when the line from Nairn (which had opened as far as Dalvey on 22 December 1857) was extended into the town; at the same time the line was extended eastwards to Elgin. The original station was closed and replaced by the one illustrated here with the opening of the line south to Boat of Garten and Aviemore on 3 August 1863. To the left are the lines from Aviemore, in the centre are the lines towards Aberdeen and on the right are the direct lines which bypassed the station. The shed was located just to the right of the area shown in the photograph. *M. A. Arnold*

Now: 26 May 1998
The station is well kept and remains in use, but only as a single platform. All traces of the line from Aviemore have gone, as has the footbridge from which the 'Then' photograph was taken. The eastbound platform remains but is out of use. The photograph was taken from the west end of the platform and shows Class 158 No 158726 leaving with the 07.30 service from Aberdeen to Inverness. The train, pictured amongst the gorse bushes, makes quite a contrast with the neat appearance of the scene 42 years ago. The Boat of Garten line was closed completely on 18 October 1965 with the exception of a short line at Forres which was retained to serve Dallas Dhu until 21 May 1967. *Author*

Now: 24 May 1998
The station at Kinloss was to close on 3 May 1965; freight facilities were withdrawn from the station on 7 November 1966. The station house and platform still exist on the eastbound side, but the line has now been singled and it is not now possible to get the elevated viewpoint achieved in 1966. The road crossing has been upgraded with the provision of automatic barriers. *Author*

Elgin

Then: Undated (pre-1923)
There were two stations at Elgin: this shows the Highland Railway station looking west. It shows well the general layout at this point with the long platform on the north side which connected both stations. The first station to serve Elgin was the future GNSR station, which opened, with the line to Lossiemouth, on 10 August 1852. The line from Forres to Elgin opened under the auspices of the Inverness & Aberdeen Junction Railway on 25 March 1858; it was extended eastwards to Keith on 18 August 1858. *Ian Allan Library*

Now: 26 May 1998
The tracks have been rationalised although the basic layout remains unchanged. The station has been modernised and is well used, although the platform no longer connects with the (now closed) ex-GNoSR station. The line on the right is the stub of the closed GNoSR line, which remains to serve the goods yard. *Author*

Fort George

Then: 1933
This was another Highland Railway branch which connected with the Inverness-Aberdeen main line, this time at Gollanfield Junction, 9.5 miles east of Inverness. The 1.5-mile line, which had no intermediate stations, opened on 1 July 1899. This view shows the relatively simple terminus in Fort George; like a number of other branches, the station was located some distance from the settlement it purported to serve. *Ian Allan Library*

Burghead

Then: 12 September 1958
Burghead was situated on the 7.5-mile long branch which linked Alves, on the Inverness-Aberdeen main line, with Hopeman. The first station at Burghead opened on 23 December 1862; this was replaced by a second station, that illustrated here, when the line was extended to Hopeman on 10 October 1892. By the date of this photograph, passenger services over the branch had already ceased — on 14 September 1931 but the line remained open for freight as far as Burghead; the section to Hopeman closed completely on 30 December 1957. Here, ex-CR '812' class 0-6-0 No 57620 is pictured working the branch freight.
H. D. Bowtell

Now: 24 May 1998
Freight continued to serve Burghead until 7 November 1966, when services were cut back to a point just south of the station to serve a grain processor at Roseilse. Today the station still stands, as do the remains of the platform. The road bridge in the background of the 'Then' view has, however, disappeared, and the road now crosses the site on the level. The track serving Roseilse terminates behind the photographer; the line still receives deliveries by rail, normally on Wednesdays. *Author*

Now: 24 May 1998
Passenger services over the Fort George branch ceased on 5 April 1943 and freight was to be withdrawn on 11 August 1958. The station area has now been redeveloped and houses built on the site. I calculated that the 'Then' picture was taken from what is today the garden of house No 2. Deep in the undergrowth to the left, the owner told me, there was still a rail. *Author*

Inverness station (south)

Then: July 1955
It was on 21 September 1854 that the construction of the 15-mile Inverness-Nairn line commenced. It was opened on 5 November 1855; the route was subsequently extended to Aberdeen (by the GNoSR). The line from Perth via Aviemore, Dava and Forres opened in 1863; the south end of Inverness station, illustrated here, served these workings from Platforms 1 to 4. Class 5 No 45123, plus another member of the class is seen preparing to depart with a train to Perth routed via Carr Bridge. The Highland Railway's locomotive works were constructed on a site to the right of the picture, after Lochgorm had been drained. *Ian Allan Library*

Now: 24 May 1998
Inverness was resignalled and the track rationalised in the mid-1980s; this work saw the replacement of the Inverness area boxes at Welsh's Bridge (105 levers), Millburn Junction (51 levers) and Rose Street (45 levers). Unfortunately, it also resulted in the demolition of the fine gantries to the south of the station, which has no doubt increased the efficiency of the operation but meant that the scene has lost much of its railway interest. However, this particular view has not altered all that much, and shows Class 158s Nos 158723 and 158711 stabled in the station on a Sunday morning. The photograph was taken from the south end of Platform 2. *Author*

Inverness shed

Then: 9 June 1957
This used to be a splendid shed for photography. It was built in 1864 with a 21-road, three-quarter segment roundhouse, with this extremely impressive Doric-style disguised water tower. A very fine view of the shed and Needlefield Carriage & Wagon sidings used to be obtained from the path up to the trees on the right of the photograph; unfortunately, this is now obscured by trees. On this occasion, Perth-based Class 5 No 44924, together with local Caledonian McIntosh Class 812 0-6-0 No 57597 were present. The roundhouse was full and contained two Caledonian 'Pugs', which had been introduced in 1885 and which worked the harbour branch. In 1935, 43 locomotives were allocated to Inverness, 91 in 1944 and 48 in January 1960, of which 33 were Class 5MTs. The steam shed was originally coded 29H in the Perth Area, becoming 32A in 1940 and finally 60A under British Railways. *Author*

Inverness station (north)

Then: July 1955
The north side of the station consists of Platforms 5 to 7 and was opened for services to Dingwall, 18 miles away, on 11 June 1862. It was not until 1874 that services started to Wick, a distance of 161 miles by rail but only 80 as the crow flies. Through services to the far north line used to use the avoiding line and reverse into the station; this operation still occurs when specials are run to Kyle of Lochalsh and other far north destinations from the south. Until closure, this manoeuvre was controlled by Rose Street Bridge Junction box. As can be seen, these platforms were built on a sharp curve. On this occasion, Class 5 No 45192 is waiting to depart with a train for the north. Note the tablet catchers on the cab side. *Ian Allan Library*

Now: 24 May 1998
A Sunday morning sees Class 156 units Nos 156499 and 156458 in Platforms 5 and 6 ready for the first Monday morning services to Kyle of Lochalsh and Wick/Thurso. In the background are Class 158s for the Aberdeen and Perth trains. There are still facilities at Inverness to turn steam locomotives on their rare visits by use of the triangle. Over the past few years, Inverness town centre has become very congested with traffic, although encouragingly the trains continue to be well used. *Author*

Now: 24 May 1998
After the demise of steam in the area in mid-1961, the shed was demolished. The site then provided space for an extension to the existing cattle market. By 1998, the old cattle market looked derelict and the site looked ripe for development, although a car boot sale was preparing to open at 09.00 in the background. *Author*

Muir of Ord

Then: 1911
This superb photograph was taken in 1911. The locomotive is Highland Railway No 21, one of the 'Barney' Class 0-6-0s built by Dubs in 1902; this locomotive lasted until February 1949. Notice the station nameboard proclaiming 'Muir of Ord Junction, change here for Black Isle line to Fortrose'. The dress of the passengers is also worth a close look. The line from Inverness to Dingwall opened on 11 June 1862 and Muir of Ord became a junction with the opening of the Fortrose branch on 1 February 1894. *Ian Allan Library*

Now: 22 May 1998
The station buildings have been demolished and only a very basic shelter is provided on the old down platform; the up platform is, I believe, only used when trains pass. Here the 'Royal Scotsman' arrives empty from Dingwall, headed by Class 37/4 No 37428 in a special livery. The train was waiting to collect its passengers, who had been visiting Dunrobin Castle on a dismal day. *Author*

Fortrose

Then: 14 August 1959
The 13.5-mile long branch to Fortrose left the main line at Muir of Ord. The line opened throughout on 1 February 1894 and, by the date of this photograph, had already lost its passenger services (on 1 October 1951). This picture shows ex-CR McIntosh Class 812 0-6-0 No 57594 taking water at the terminus whilst working the local pick-up freight. *D. Capper*

Now: 22 May 1998
Freight services over the Fortrose branch ceased on 13 June 1960. It was extremely difficult to locate the exact position from which the 'Then' photograph was taken, but, with the help of a long-time resident of Fortrose, we decided that this was the spot. As can be seen, the whole of the station area has been redeveloped. *Author*

Dingwall

Then: July 1955
Dingwall is the point where the line to Kyle of Lochalsh leaves the main line to Wick and heads off west. The junction is just to the north of Dingwall station. The line from Inverness to Dingwall was opened on 11 June 1862 by the Inverness & Ross-shire Railway. It was extended from Dingwall to Invergordon on 25 May 1863. The Kyle line opened from Dingwall as far as Strome Ferry on 19 August 1870. Dingwall was served by a small locomotive shed, which was situated to the south of the station. Here an Inverness-allocated Stanier Class 5, No 44788, has just arrived on the 9.40am service from Wick. The distance from Dingwall to Wick is 142.75 miles. *Ian Allan Library (K2659)*

Now: 22 May 1998
There have been some changes over the past 43 years, although both Far North and Kyle lines remain open. The signals have gone and the bay platform at the north end is no longer in use. The road bridge has only recently been replaced. Overall, however, the condition of the station seems better than it was in 1955. Class 37/4 No 37428, painted in a special maroon livery to match the 'Royal Scotsman' train, is pictured arriving with its service. The passengers were then taken by coach to visit Dunrobin Castle, before re-embarking on the train at Muir of Ord in the evening. *Author*

Achnasheen

Then: 29 August 1958
The station is about four miles short of being the midpoint between Kyle and Dingwall and has always been one of the major passing points on the line. It opened, along with the line as far as Strome Ferry, on 19 August 1870 under the auspices of the Dingwall & Skye Railway. This view, taken looking westwards, shows the line stretching off towards the summit at Luib.
Neil Caplan

Achanalt

Then: July 1971
This remote station, which was opened by the Dingwall & Skye Railway at the same time as the line from Dingwall to Strome Ferry on 19 August 1870, is situated to the north of Loch Achanalt and between the summits of Luib to the west and Corriemullie to the east. It is located 21.5 miles from Dingwall and 6.25 miles east of Achnasheen.
Andrew Muckley

Now: 22 May 1998
The station remains open today as a request halt for services between Kyle and Inverness. The old station building has gone, to be replaced by a small shelter. The house behind has had its roof extended, but otherwise seems to be largely unchanged over 27 years. The road, which is located behind the house, has, however, had considerable amounts of money spent on it in recent years, despite the relative paucity of traffic.
Author

Now: 22 May 1998
The station remains open although freight facilities have been long withdrawn; sidings, however, remain extant, and these appear to be used by Railtrack. No doubt, if the need arose, the sidings could be used for timber or other traffic. The water column and signals have gone, whilst the station building is now privately owned. The building suffered a recent small fire in the cafe. The prestigious 'Royal Scotsman' train passes through heading towards Keith where it was to be stabled for the night. The train is headed by Class 37/4 No 37428, which was painted in a special maroon livery to match the train's coaching stock. *Author*

Strathcarron

Then: 7 April 1971
This picture shows an Inverness-Kyle of Lochalsh goods calling at the station headed by Birmingham RCW Type 2 (later Class 26) No D5336 (later No 26036) and Sulzer Type 2 (later Class 24) No D5128 (later No 24128). The station, which is located at the east end of Loch Carron, was opened on 19 August 1870. *Derek Cross*

Now: 23 May 1998
Strathcarron remains open and is still used as a passing place for trains between Kyle of Lochalsh and Achnasheen. Apart from the demolition of the signalbox and the growth of the trees on the right-hand side, little seems to have altered in the 27 years separating these two photographs. The 10.45 service from Inverness, formed of Class 156 No 156458, is waiting for the 11.45 service from Kyle to pass. *Author*

Kyle of Lochalsh (shed site)

Then: Undated (1950s)
The old steam shed at Kyle of Lochalsh was about a quarter of a mile inland from the passenger station. This photograph shows 'Clan Goods' No 57955 ready to back into the station, with sister locomotive No 57956 inside the shed. Both locomotives were withdrawn in the summer of 1952. One of the ex-CR 0-4-4Ts was usually the station pilot, but Stanier Class 5s were the normal motive power for the last 20 years of steam operation until the arrival of the diesels in the early 1960s. *C. C. B. Herbert*

Now: 23 May 1998
The site has now been redeveloped and little now remains to show that the shed once stood here, although as recently as eight years ago the turntable still existed. The running line is just to the left of the photograph in a rock cutting. *Author*

Kyle of Lochalsh

Then: August 1954
This view records a very busy scene at the terminus of the line from
Dingwall. A Stanier Class 5 is ready to leave with a train for
Inverness, whilst the ferry to Stornoway stands by the quayside. The
extension of the line from Strome Ferry to Kyle of Lochalsh, with

intermediate stations at Plockton and Duirinish, opened on
2 November 1897. Also worthy of note is the amount of freight
traffic visible. *Eric Treacy*

Now: 23 May 1998
The station has not changed greatly over
the past 40 years, although the motive
power has. Here Class 156 No 156477
Highland Festival is seen in the station
ready to form the 11.45 service to
Inverness. After many years, freight
activity has returned to the port, the line
on the right, from which loading can
take place, having been installed in
1998. I am afraid that, on my visits to
Kyle of Lochalsh, the Isle of Skye is
usually covered in cloud, as was the
case here, with the result that the
backdrop looks very different.
Author

Invergordon

Then: 11 April 1973
Invergordon is situated 31.25 miles north of Inverness and used to see a considerable amount of freight traffic in connection with the North Sea oil and gas industry. The line from Dingwall to Invergordon opened on 25 May 1863; it was extended from Invergordon north to Meikle Ferry (from where a ferry connection to Dornoch operated; once the line to Bonar Bridge was opened, the connection to Dornoch was transferred to Bonar Bridge and Meikle Ferry station closed in 1869) on 1 June 1864. Here Class 24 No D5119 (later No 24119) is pictured heading towards Inverness with the 11.25 service from Wick. *Peter W. Robinson*

Now: 22 May 1998
The line remains open, although freight traffic to Invergordon has ceased. Today there are only the two through lines. The station suffered a serious fire in recent years and has been demolished save for the entrance area on the up side. This is a slightly different viewpoint, as a result of a wide-angle lens being used, but notice how the bushes have grown on the embankment over the years.
Author

Tain shed

Then: 9 June 1957
The shed at Tain was situated just south of the station alongside the main line. The first shed opened here in June 1864 and was a wooden structure. This burnt down and was replaced by the stone structure illustrated in this view. As it was a Sunday, all the locomotives were dead, as there were no train or other services in this part of Scotland at this time on the Sabbath. Visible are three ex-CR Pickersgill 4-4-0s well coaled ready for the following day's duties, with No 54470 closest to the camera. The other locomotives included No 54496. *Author*

Now: 25 May 1998
This is a slightly different view as there was nothing to indicate where the shed had once stood. The cemetery, however, is still present, albeit today well hidden by the vegetation. *Author*

Ardgay

Then: 1939
Known originally as 'Bonar Bridge', the line from Meikle Ferry to this point opened on 1 October 1864. It was to be a further four years until the line was further extended northwards to Golspie (on 13 April 1868). This view shows the down 'Orcadian' entering the station, having completed some 57.5 miles of its 161-mile trip to Wick. The motive power is provided by a Stanier Class 5. As can be seen, Bonar Bridge was a passing place. *Ian Allan Library*

Tain

Then: April 1959
This fine station opened on 1 June 1864
with the extension of the line north from
Invergordon. It is located 44 miles north
of Inverness. Here ex-CR Pickersgill
'113' class 4-4-0 No 54470, allocated to
Inverness but no doubt sub-shedded at
this time to Tain, is seen ready to leave
with a local train to Inverness.
R. T. Hughes

Now: 25 May 1998
The station remains open for services to
and from the Far North. The 11.45 from
Wick and the 12.02 from Thurso, which
combined at Georgemas Junction, pass
on the up line on their way to Inverness.
The platforms are today much longer
than required for the two- or four-car
trains that form the regular services over
the line and few excursions now call. All
freight traffic from this location has
ceased. *Author*

Now: 26 May 1998
The station remains a passing place. The
station building and platforms have
altered little in 60 years, although the
goods yard has vanished. Bonar Bridge
was actually in Ardgay, being situated
about two miles from Bonar Bridge itself
(and on the opposite side of the Kyle of
Sutherland), and so it is not surprising
that British Rail renamed the station
'Ardgay' on 2 May 1977. This busy
scene shows the 15.44 Wick-Inverness
train, formed of Class 156 No 156474,
leaving the station whilst passing the
17.15 Inverness-Wick train. The latter
was made up of sister unit No 156477,
which had already made a trip to Thurso
and return earlier in the day. Ardgay was
the point where the crews of the two
trains changed over. *Author*

Culrain

Then: 26 July 1955
The 9.45am Wick-Inverness train, headed by Inverness-allocated Class 5 No 45192, picks up the single-line token whilst passing through the station. This station, located 60.75 miles north of Inverness, was on the section of line, from Bonar Bridge to Golspie, which opened on 13 April 1868. *P. L. Sibley*

Now: 26 May 1998
All signs of the former up side have gone and only a single platform survives. As one can see, the location has got very enclosed by trees. *Author*

The Mound

Then: 23 April 1952
The Mound was the junction for the branch to Dornoch, the line of which is seen to the right of the picture. The station opened here on 13 April 1868, 34 years before the branch to Dornoch opened (on 2 June 1902). In the photograph an up train from Wick, headed by Stanier Class 5 No 45479, pauses at the station. The locomotive is in the early British Railways livery. *H. C. Casserley*

Now: 25 May 1998
The branch to Dornoch lost both its passenger and freight services on 13 June 1960, at which time the junction station was also closed. Today, all that remains are the up platform and the fine station house, which is now privately owned. The main line has also been singled and most passengers on board the Class 156s that traverse the line will be unaware that a station or junction ever existed at this point. *Author*

Dornoch

Then: July 1955

This was the terminus of the 7.75-mile branch which left the main line at The Mound, 80.5 miles north of Inverness. The branch had three intermediate stations and opened on 2 June 1902, as the Dornoch Light Railway. Trains over the line were usually mixed, with one passenger coach, and the line was the preserve of the lovely little Highland Railway '25' class 0-4-4Ts, especially Nos 55051 and 55053, which lasted until 1956 and 1957 respectively. No 55053 was fully lined out in black livery following its last overhaul at St Rollox Works in July 1955 and it was destined to become the last ex-HR locomotive to remain in service. These little tanks were replaced by two Great Western '16xx' 0-6-0PTs, Nos 1646 and 1649, which lasted until services ceased. Here No 55053 is pictured ready to leave for The Mound. *Ian Allan Library (K2655)*

Now: 25 May 1998

Today, following the line's complete closure on 13 June 1960, the station area is well maintained and the platform still survives. The station, however, has a new function; it now serves as a fast-food take-away. *Author*

Brora

Then: 1957
This passing point is situated some 90.25 miles north of Inverness.
The line through Brora from Golspie to Helmsdale opened on
19 June 1871 as part of the Duke of Sutherland's Railway. One of the
ex-CR Pickersgill Class 72 4-4-0s is illustrated piloting Stanier
Class 5 No 44991 into the station at the head of a northbound train.
C. Lawson Kerr

Now: 25 May 1998
Apart from the signalling, the loss of the old-style nameboard and the
reduced number of passengers, the scene at Brora has not changed a
great deal over the past 41 years. The station remains a passing point
for services over the line north of Inverness. Here the 07.00 service
from Inverness to Thurso, formed on this occasion by Class 156
No 156477 *Highland Festival* (the name can be seen on the side of
the unit), is pictured arriving on a stormy morning, having taken 2hr
11min from Inverness. The journey included 12 intermediate stops
before the train reached Brora. *Author*

Helmsdale

Then: 9 June 1957
The railway reached this point from the south on 19 July 1871 and it remained the terminus of the line for three years until the section onwards to Thurso and Wick opened on 28 July 1874. The shed was located at the north end of the down platform and was the main shed between Inverness and Wick, providing pilot locomotives in both directions. The shed was also responsible for the locomotives working the Dornoch branch, which was ultimately worked by two ex-Great Western 0-6-0PTs. This photograph was taken on a Sunday evening during the summer of 1957 and it shows an ex-CR Pickersgill '72' class 4-4-0 No 54495 alongside Stanier Class 5 No 45319, which was being prepared for the 1.45am freight to Wick. *Author*

Now: 25 May 1998
Following the replacement of steam on the lines north of Inverness, it would appear that diesel locomotives were stabled at Helmsdale until it closed completely in 1961. Today, the shed area has been landscaped, but the turntable pit to the back of where I took the picture can still be seen. The station has altered little, although the buildings are not now used for passengers and the signalbox appears to be used by Railtrack to store equipment. Both platforms are still used. *Author*

Kildonan

Then: Undated
This remote station, situated 9.5 miles northwest of Helmsdale, was opened on 28 July 1874. The date of the photograph is not recorded, but it was obviously taken from the carriage window of a northbound train and shows part of the footbridge and shed on the southbound platform.
Ian Allan Library

Now: 25 May 1998
I have stood on the opposite platform to show more of the general scene for this 'Now' photograph. As can be seen, the footbridge has gone and the ex-northbound platform is now out of use. The shed, however, remains *in situ* . There are currently three trains per day in either direction, which call at this station by request. *Author*

Georgemas Junction (looking south)

Then: 6 July 1955
This is the most northerly junction in the British Isles. The railway station opened at this desolate location on 28 July 1874 as part of the Sutherland & Caithness Railway. Its importance over the years has been because of the fact that it is the point at which trains to Wick and Thurso from Inverness split into two portions. Here, a Thurso-bound train is pictured ready to leave behind an ex-Caledonian Railway 0-4-4T. At this time there was obviously a fair amount of livestock traffic. The turntable was situated just to the right of the signalbox. *K. R. Pirt*

Now: 25 May 1998
The 07.00 Inverness-Thurso train is shown arriving; the train is formed of Class 156 No 156477 *Highland Festival*. This train connected with a Thurso-Wick train which was already in the platform and will then reverse and travel the 6.75 miles to Thurso. The unit then would form the 12.12 service back to Inverness, combining with the other unit, which formed the 11.45 service from Wick. The two units combined to form a four-car set for the journey southwards to Inverness. There are sidings just to the east of the station and there has been a limited amount of freight recently; however, passenger levels are probably relatively low. *Author*

Wick

Then: 8 July 1958
Wick is approximately 749 miles from Euston. The line from Helmsdale to Wick opened on 28 July 1874. This photograph shows ex-Caledonian Railway 'Dunalastair IV' class 4-4-0 No 54439 shunting vans behind the signalbox. The lines on the extreme right went to more sidings and to the locomotive shed. The latter, in BR days, was allocated code 60D. *K. L. Cook*

Georgemas Junction
(Inverness end)

Then: Undated (c1910)
This photograph shows the view of
Georgemas Junction looking east. It
portrays a train ready to leave for
Thurso behind what appears to be one of
the HR 'Strath' class 4-4-0s, whilst on
the right is an Inverness-bound train,
hauled by one of the famous HR 'Loch'
class 4-4-0s, probably No 199 *Loch Insh*
which was built by Dubs in 1896. The
turntable and signalbox are clearly
shown. *F. Moore/Ian Allan Library*

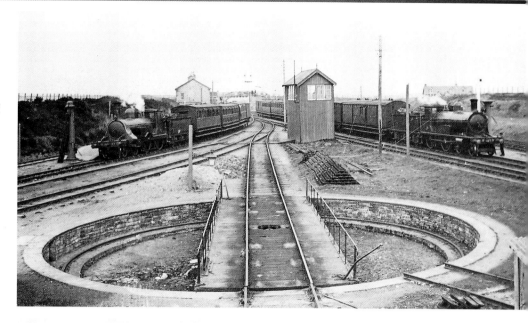

Now: 25 May 1998
Although the track has been rationalised
and both the signalbox and turntable
have gone, the scene at Georgemas
Junction is not unrecognisable almost 90
years on. Services continue both to Wick
and to Thurso, as well as southwards to
Inverness. *Author*

Now: 25 May 1998
Steam finished operating over the line to
Wick in 1959 and the shed closed
in August 1962. As can be seen, there
are still limited sidings. The country end
of the platform, nearest the camera, sees
little use today other than for the
occasional loco-hauled special. On this
occasion a two-car Class 156 unit,
No 156446, is in the station ready to
leave on the 11.45 service to Inverness.
This will combine at Georgemas
Junction with the 12.02 from Thurso.
Author

Lybster

Then: Undated (c1910)

Unfortunately, this 'Then' photograph is undated, but it must date to around 1910 or earlier judging from the dresses of the ladies on the platform. The 13.75-mile branch which headed south from Wick was opened on 1 July 1903 as the Wick & Lybster Light Railway. Lybster was, until the opening of the Channel Tunnel, the furthest point it was possible to reach without interruption by rail from London. The line possessed four intermediate stations; these had the delightful names of Thrumster, Ulbster, Mid Clyth and Occumster. The small shed at Lybster can be seen on the right in this view.
Ian Allan Library (7872)

Now: 25 May 1998

The line between Wick and Lybster was closed completely on 1 April 1944. As can be seen, the station building is still extant, although this is the first occasion when producing a book of this nature that I have discovered a former station in use as a golf clubhouse. Little else remains at Lybster, although the old railway land has not been redeveloped. The remains of the trackbed can still be clearly seen at several places from the road to Wick. *Author*

Thurso

Then: 10 September 1958
This view is from the bridge at the south end of the station and shows the railway layout to advantage. Inside the small shed in the centre of the picture is a Stanier 2-6-2T, No 40150, which was allocated to the branch in the late 1950s. The line from Georgemas Junction to Thurso opened on 28 July 1874, at the same time as the line from Wick to Helmsdale. *H. D. Bowtell*

Now: 25 May 1998
Apart from the lifting of the line to the shed, the general scene at Thurso has changed little since 1958. This photograph is taken with a medium telephoto lens as the bushes on the left would have obscured a great deal of the view with a standard lens. Class 156 No 156477 *Highland Festival* is in the station prior to forming the 12.02 service to Inverness. Had it not been for the traffic to the nuclear power station at Dounreay, which has now ceased, it is probable that the branch — indeed all of the line north of Inverness — would have closed. *Author*

North British Railway

Of the main Scottish railway companies, the largest was the North British. With operations stretching from Carlisle to Aberdeen and from Berwick to Mallaig, the railway came to dominate railway history in the Scottish borders, Fife and much of the central industrial belt. The track mileage operated by the NBR — at 1,378 — made it the fifth largest of all the pre-Grouping companies. History, however, could have been very different if the Edinburgh & Glasgow Railway had progressed, as originally planned, into merger with the Caledonian Railway rather than the NBR. Moreover, few of the major pre-Grouping companies suffered the fate of seeing another company operating the major express services over its own main line as was the case of the North Eastern running north of Berwick to Edinburgh.

On the other hand, the NBR was involved directly in two of the three main lines linking Scotland with England and, through ownership of a short stretch of line to the east of Glasgow, an indirect role in the West Coast main line as well.

As a result of the NBR's take over of the earlier Edinburgh & Dalkeith Railway in 1845, the company was, therefore, operating trains before the formal launch of its own main line from Berwick to Edinburgh on 22 June 1846. From these beginnings the NBR was to expand considerably over the next few decades. The first section of the Waverley route — from Edinburgh to Hawick — was to open on 1 November 1849; it was to be completed through to Carlisle on 1 July 1862 (although it was a great commercial success until the opening of the Midland's line to Carlisle in the 1870s). The NBR gained access to the region north of the Firth of Forth with amalgamation with the Edinburgh, Perth & Dundee Railway on 1 August 1862. Railway traffic between Edinburgh and Dundee initially required the use of two ferries, but this was to be obviated by the end of the century through the construction of two of the greatest railway bridges constructed in the UK — the Tay Bridge and the Forth Bridge.

The amalgamation with the EP&DR was one of two major mergers which affected the development of the NBR; the second was that with the Edinburgh & Glasgow Railway. This company, which had opened on 22 February 1842, had long been regarded as being in the CR's camp; however, failure to forge an amalgamation resulted in the operating agreement terminating on 1 August 1864 with the NBR taking over. The NBR, through these arrangements, thus acquired workshops at Burntisland (ex-EP&DR) and Cowlairs (ex-E&GR) as well as its own facilities at St Margarets in Edinburgh. Gradually, Cowlairs came to dominate and many of the classic locomotive designs produced by the NBR were to emerge from the Glasgow works.

Following the completion of the first Tay Bridge in 1879, the NBR acquired a share from the Caledonian Railway in the line linking Dundee with Arbroath; the Dundee & Arbroath Joint, as the line became known, was to form an integral part of the NBR's contribution to the East Coast main line. Unfortunately, the triumph of the Tay Bridge's opening was destroyed along with the bridge when the latter collapsed in a gale in December 1879; the replacement bridge, now built to double track, opened in 1887. This was to be followed by the opening of the Forth Bridge which, whilst owned and constructed by a joint committee, was clearly used primarily by the NBR.

By the end of the 19th century, the NBR was largely complete. The early years of the 20th century did see, however, the construction of a number of new lines. Of these, the most important was the extension of the West Highland line from Fort William to Mallaig, which opened in 1901. In 1907 the NBR began operating over the line from Spean Bridge to Fort Augustus. Originally, the Highland Railway, fearful that the NBR would use the line as a means of gaining access to the Highlands, had operated the route, despite the fact that it was separate from the rest of the HR system. Never successful, NBR suspended its own services in 1911 before restoring them in 1913.

The NBR passed to the newly created London & North Eastern Railway in 1923, as one of the two Scottish companies taken over by the LNER. Cowlairs was to build its final locomotive in 1924, although NBR influence was to survive in that William Whitelaw was to be chairman of the new company. As elsewhere, the period of the 'Big Four' saw the closure to passenger services of a number of lines. These included the route from Balloch to Balfron (on 1 October 1934), Banavie Pier (on 4 September 1939), Bathgate Upper to Morningside (1 May 1950), Dolphinton-Leadburn (1 April 1933), Charlestown-Dunfermline (1 November 1926), Dalkeith-Millerhill (5 January 1942), Fort Augustus- Spean Bridge (1 December 1933), Glencorse-Millerhill (1 May 1933), Gullane-Longniddry (12 September 1932) and Lauder-Fountainhall Junction (12 September 1932). Also to disappear during the interwar years were many of the classic locomotive designs produced by the NBR; amongst the types to succumb were the stylish Reid Atlantics. The last of the class, No 875 *Midlothian*, was withdrawn and sent for scrap. However, instructions for its preservation were received at Cowlairs with the result that the locomotive was resurrected and re-entered service. This was not to be the end of the story; No 875 was to be withdrawn again in the early years of World War 2 and, with the drive for scrap metal, there was to be no second reprieve.

The period of Nationalisation was to see much of the erstwhile NBR network close. The most dramatic closures affected the lines serving the Scottish borders, culminating in the complete closure of the Waverley route in January 1969. The Edinburgh suburban lines have also disappeared along with many of these serving Fife and the central industrial belt. Not all was negative, however, as the closure of the line to Bathgate was reversed with services being restored on 12 May 1986. Currently, passenger services operate over the East Coast main line from Berwick to Dundee via both the Forth and Tay bridges, between Edinburgh and Glasgow and over the West Highland line from Glasgow to Mallaig. Other ex-NBR routes retaining passenger services include the line from Ladybank to Perth, Inverkeithing to Thornton Junction (via Dunfermline and Cowdenbeath), the Bathgate branch and a number of suburban routes in and around Glasgow. The Bo'ness line is now preserved by the Scottish Railway Preservation Society whilst sections of other lines remain for freight traffic.

As the new Millennium approaches, there are strong possibilities that more of the ex-NBR network may yet reappear. There are strong proposals for the reopening of various lines — such as that through Alloa and the southern section of the Waverley route — to freight traffic whilst a scheme for reopening the northern section of the Waverley route for commuter traffic into Edinburgh is also gaining ground.

Reston

Then: 15 July 1961
In the days before yellow warning panels at the front of diesel locomotives, Gateshead-allocated Type 4 (Class 40) No D256 departs from Reston with a down express. The station opened on 22 June 1846 and, with the opening of the line to Duns on 15 August 1849, was to become a junction. A number of freight wagons in the yard indicates that at this date, Reston still provided freight facilities. *Author*

Now: 28 July 1998
I had to take this picture slightly more head-on than that of 37 years ago as bushes had grown on the embankment. A picture taken in 1989 showed no signs of any bushes at the side of the track; it is quite amazing how quickly the undergrowth seems to have taken off all over the Railtrack network when it hardly appeared to grow at all for 20 years after the end of steam. Perhaps it was a case that BR kept it under control and such activity is not considered necessary by Railtrack? Passenger services on the branch to Duns ceased on 10 September 1951 and the line closed completely on 7 November 1966. Reston station itself closed on 4 May 1964 and freight facilities were withdrawn two years later. Here a Class 91 heads north with a service from King's Cross to Edinburgh past the site of the station; note that the goods shed remains intact in the background. *Author*

Eyemouth

Then: 15 July 1961
The two-mile long branch from Burnmouth, on the East Coast main line, to Eyemouth opened on 13 April 1891. The line had lost its passenger services for the first time on 13 August 1948, but these had been restored on 29 June 1949. Here Tweedmouth-allocated Class J39 0-6-0 No 64917 was in charge of the single-coach train and is pictured ready to depart for Burnmouth. *Author*

Now: 28 July 1998
Passenger services over the Eyemouth branch were withdrawn on 5 February 1962 and the line closed completely at the same time. The station used to be on a ledge between the road above and the railway below; as can be seen, the station site has been levelled and a car park built. Although still in use, the church in the background appears to have all its windows boarded up. *Author*

Grantshouse

Then: 13 July 1961
On this occasion the station still looked as though it was expecting to receive passengers, although it had in fact been closed since 18 June 1951. Note the water column alongside the signalbox. Gateshead-allocated Type 4 No D273 heads south with an up express. *Author*

Now: 28 July 1998
Freight facilities from Grantshouse were withdrawn in 1964. Although the station and box are long gone, up and down loops are still provided, as are a couple of sidings on the up side. The 07.30 service from King's Cross to Edinburgh heads north. *Author*

Cockburnspath

Then: 13 July 1961
Although the station had closed to passenger services a decade earlier — on 18 June 1951 — all is still in place as a virtually brand-new Type 4 (later Class 40) No D261 passes with an up express. As can be seen, freight facilities were provided at the station, although these were to be withdrawn on 25 January 1965. The North British Railway main line from Edinburgh to Berwick opened on 22 June 1846. *Author*

Now: 28 July 1998
Electrification has appeared and all traces of the former station have disappeared. The 08.00 service from King's Cross rushes north at high speed *en route* to Edinburgh. The skyline has altered with the arrival of the Torness nuclear power station. *Author*

Dunbar

Then: 10 September 1970
The station at Dunbar opened on 22 June 1846. It was built on a loop from the East Coast main line with an up and down platform as illustrated in this picture. *J. Scrace*

Now: 28 July 1998
At the time of electrification, the down platform was removed as was the footbridge. This picture shows the East Coast main line on the right and the new track layout. *Author*

North Berwick shed

Then: 1 September 1956
The branch engine, Class V1 2-6-2T No 67670, receives a final polish at North Berwick shed before setting off to the station to pick up its stock for the next Edinburgh train. It is pictured outside the shed; North Berwick was a sub-shed of St Margarets. *Author*

North Berwick

Then: 30 August 1956
The North Berwick branch opened throughout on 17 June 1850. It runs for 4.75 miles from its junction with the East Coast main line at Drem. Back in 1956 the regular branch locomotive was kept in spotless condition by the local sub-shed. Class V1 2-6-2T No 67670 departs from the station with a service for Edinburgh (Waverley). *Author*

Now: 28 July 1998
The goods yard and original station have been obliterated, and all that is left is the one platform and the single electrified line, although the area is well kept. The current service is operated by ex-Great Eastern section Class 305 EMUs, although these are scheduled to be replaced by more modern units in the near future. *Author*

Now: 28 July 1998
Nothing remains, except the road bridge and the single track. New houses have also appeared at the top of the embankment. *Author*

Duns

Then: 24 July 1963
The line from Reston to Duns opened on 15 August 1849 and was extended from Duns to Earlston, under the auspices of the Berwickshire Railway, on 16 November 1863. Through passenger services over the line beyond Duns through to Ravenswood Junction on the Waverley route ceased on 12 August 1948 as a result of serious flooding in the Borders. The Reston-Duns section lost its passenger services on 10 September 1951. By the date of this photograph, the line had already been singled through the station and the remaining freight services were scarce. *J. Spencer Gilks*

Now: 28 July 1998
The line from Reston closed completely on 7 November 1966. The former station is now the building on the left of this picture, but the rest of the site has now become occupied by an engineering company, John Thornburn & Sons. Although this was an ex-NBR line, there was still an ex-North Eastern Railway trespass notice on the site when this picture was taken. *Author*

Leaderfoot Viaduct

Then: 9 July 1961
This must be one of the most attractive viaducts in the country. It carried the Ravenswood Junction-Reston line over the River Tweed just to the north of Newton St Boswells. It was built on the section of line, from Ravenswood Junction to Earlston opened on 2 October 1865. The remainder of the line, from Earlston to Duns, had been completed in 1863; the two-year delay in the opening of this section was as a result of building this 19-arch structure. In July 1961 the RCTS operated a tour over a number of lines in the Scottish Borders, including the remaining section of the through route — to Greenlaw — which was by this date freight only. The train was hauled by preserved No 256 *Glen Douglas* and by Class J37 0-6-0 No 64624. *Author*

Greenlaw

Then: 9 July 1961
This was one of the intermediate stations on the line between Reston and Ravenswood Junction. On this occasion, the West Riding branch of the RCTS had organised a special railtour over a number of Borders lines; for this section of the tour motive power was provided by the preserved 'D34' No 256 *Glen Douglas* and Class J37 No 64624. The line from Duns to Earlston opened on 16 November 1863. Passenger services over the route were suspended on 13 August 1948 following flooding in the area; they were never resumed. The line between Greenlaw and Duns was to close completely at the same time. *Author*

Now: 28 July 1998
The station is now a private house and this shed, built on the trackbed, is owned by a local tractor repairer. Following the closure of the through route on 13 August 1948, Greenlaw was the terminus of the freight-only branch from Ravenswood Junction; it was to close completely on 19 July 1965. *Author*

Now: 27 July 1998
Although the line was to close completely between Ravenswood Junction and Greenlaw on 19 July 1965, the viaduct survives and is today in the care of Historic Scotland. A walkway has been constructed across the bridge and, unlike so many others, the view is still unrestricted with a noticeable lack of trees and bushes. A new road bridge has been built in the background, replacing the old bridge visible at a slightly lower level. *Author*

Gilnockie

Then: 1935
This was one of two intermediate
stations on the Riddings Junction-
Langholm branch, which opened on
18 April 1864. This view is taken
looking south in the direction of
Riddings Junction.
Ian Allan Library (6115)

Now: 27 July 1998
Passenger services between Riddings
Junction and Langholm ceased on
15 June 1964 and the line was to close
completely on 18 September 1967. The
station is now a private house and the
trackbed, on which I was standing to
take this photograph, has become a
muddy track. *Author*

Newcastleton (south)

Then: 8 July 1961
This picture of Haymarket-allocated
'A3' No 60057 *Ormonde* was taken
from the road bridge which crossed the
Waverley route about half a mile from
the town, which can be seen in the
background. The locomotive is working
the midday Edinburgh (Waverley)-
Carlisle local service. The 43-mile long
Border Union line from Carlisle to
Hawick, authorised in July 1859, was
opened throughout on 1 July 1862.
Author

Langholm

Then: 6 April 1963
This is the occasion of an SLS special to
the branch; the train was headed by
preserved ex-NBR 'Glen' 4-4-0 No 256
Glen Douglas. After running round the
train, the locomotive and stock posed
for photographs. Note the great variety
of hats: the passengers seem to be
wearing caps or trilbies, whilst the
inspector, visible on the footplate, has a
bowler. The seven-mile long branch
from Riddings Junction opened on
18 April 1864. *Author*

Now: 27 July 1998
Passenger services to Langholm ceased
on 15 June 1964 — an event
commemorated by a plaque on the cairn
in the centre of the photograph — and
the line was to close completely on
18 September 1967. The old station area
has now been developed. Part of it is
now a car park, as illustrated. *Author*

Now: 27 July 1998
The road bridge has been demolished
and the road now crosses the former
railway on the level — hence the
slightly different angle. The Waverley
route was to lose its passenger services
on 6 January 1969 at which time the
section of line from Hawick to
Longtown was to close completely.
Thirty years after closure, there are now
proposals that could see the Waverley
route restored in part or in whole for
timber traffic from Kielder Forest and
for tourist traffic through the Borders.
Time will, however, tell whether these
proposals succeed when the earlier
proposed preservation of the line,
immediately after closure, failed.
Author

Riccarton Junction (looking north)

Then: 10 July 1952
This view, taken looking north from the south side of the station, shows the junction with the lines from Reedsmouth and Hexham approaching the station from the south (ie to the right). The Waverley route through Riccarton opened on 1 June 1862 to passenger services along with the Border Counties line to Hexham. Both had opened on the previous 23 June to freight traffic. *Ian Allan Library*

Now: 27 July 1998
The Border Counties line between Riccarton Junction and Hexham lost its passenger services on 15 October 1956 and was to close completely between Riccarton and Bellingham on 1 September 1958. The main Waverley route lost its passenger services on 6 January 1969, at which time the section between Hawick and Longtown closed completely. As can be seen, there is now little to indicate that the railway once formed a major junction at this remote spot — which was not served by a road until after the closure of the railway. *Author*

Riccarton Junction (north)

Then: 5 January 1969
This photograph was taken from a conveniently placed signal, as 'Deltic' No D9007 *Pinza* stopped for a photo-call at the remote station with an RCTS special on the day prior to the line's official closure. The train had originated in Leeds. Apart from the station, the location also boasted a small sub-shed at the south end of the station. There was, at this time, no road access to the station, one of the few locations in the country where this was the case. *Author*

Now: 27 July 1998
The remoteness of the location is well shown in this picture taken in July 1998 when I managed to drive to the site along the now disused trackbed, which is used today as a road for the forestry business. The small building on the left stands where the station once stood and is now a small museum run by the 'Friends of Riccarton Junction'. *Author*

Whitrope Summit

Then: 8 July 1961
This is the top of the steep 11-mile long climb from Hawick. The gradient was virtually an unbroken stretch at 1 in 75 from Newcastleton, which was also about 11 miles away, to the south. A very dirty Gresley Class V2 2-6-2, No 60840, emerges from the cutting. The train is about to cross the road and pass the signalbox and isolated houses, before entering Whitrope Tunnel. Riccarton Junction is about two miles to the south. The other main summit on the Waverley route was at Falahill. *Author*

Now: 27 July 1998
The Waverley route from Carlisle to Edinburgh lost its passenger services on 6 January 1969 and the section through Whitrope was to close completely at the same time. The trackbed still survives and is today in use for forestry traffic; also still extant are the houses. On this occasion, not only was the weather inclement, but the area seemed to be suffering from a plague of bluebottles, which made it particularly unpleasant. *Author*

Hawick (south)

Then: 8 July 1961
Heaton-allocated Class V2 2-6-2 No 60835 *The Green Howard, Alexandra, Princess of Wales' Own Yorkshire Regiment* — quite a nameplate as can be seen! — has called at Hawick with a southbound service from Edinburgh (Waverley) to Carlisle. *Author*

Hawick (viewed south)

Then: 12 November 1966
The station was on a very sharp curve and was well elevated from the road below; another feature was the very tall signalbox visible in this picture of Gresley 'A4' No 60019 *Bittern*, which was working an RCTS special from Leeds. By this date, the locomotive had already passed into private ownership. The lines on the right led to the yard and locomotive shed. The future Waverley route from St Boswells to Hawick opened on 1 November 1849; the line was extended southwards to Carlisle, opening to freight on 23 June 1862 and to passenger services on 1 July 1862. *Author*

Now: 27 July 1998
Passenger services over the Waverley route ceased on 6 January 1969 at which time the line south of Hawick to Longtown closed completely. The rump of the line from Lady Victoria colliery to Hawick was to close completely on 28 April 1969. The station area has been totally redeveloped over the past 30 years and the Teviot leisure centre now occupies the old station and goods yard site. Just as there are plans for the reopening of the Waverley route's southern end for timber traffic, so there is a scheme to reopen the line north of Hawick for passenger traffic to and from Edinburgh. *Author*

Now: 27 July 1998
The area around the Teviot leisure centre, which is to the left of this view, has been very well landscaped and it is difficult to believe that this was once where the station stood. *Author*

St Boswells (looking north)

Then: July 1961
St Boswells was a major intersection on the Waverley route; to the south lay the junction with the line towards Tweedmouth whilst to the north lay Ravenswood Junction and the branch to Duns and Reston. To service these lines a small, two-road engine shed was provided at the side of the up platform. Here ex-NBR Class J37 0-6-0 No 64608 is ready to leave with a pick-up freight for Hawick. It was on 20 February 1849 that the line from Bowland Bridge to St Boswells opened to passenger traffic — it had opened for freight on 8 February 1849 — and the line was to be extended to Hawick on the following 1 November. The branch to Kelso followed on 1 June 1851 whilst the final part of the line to Reston, the Ravenswood Junction-Earlston section, followed in 1865.
J. C. Baker

Now: 27 July 1998
In amongst the undergrowth, the up platform can just be traced. The locomotive shed still stands and is in use by a fuel oil company, Baxter & Johnson. Passenger services to Kelso ceased on 15 June 1964, those to Duns having ceased in 1948. The Kelso line was to close completely on 1 April 1968; that to Greenlaw had closed completely on 19 July 1965. Passenger services through St Boswells on the Waverley route ceased on 6 January 1969 and this section was to close completely on 28 April 1969.
Author

Roxburgh

Then: Undated (c1950s)
This was another of the three intermediate stations on the ex-NBR section from St Boswells to Kelso and was the point where the Jedburgh branch headed south. The St Boswells-Kelso line opened on 17 June 1850 whilst the Jedburgh branch followed on 17 July 1856. This view looking east shows the Jedburgh branch curving around to the right (ie south). Passenger services to Jedburgh ceased on 13 August 1948 as a result of the serious floods in the Scottish borders; they were never resumed although the line was restored for freight traffic. *C. J. B. Sanderson*

Rutherford

Then: 1963
This remote station was one of the three intermediate stations on the St Boswells-Kelso line, which opened on 17 June 1850. The somewhat Spartan facilities of the station, with its single platform, are all too evident. *Ian Allan Library*

Now: 27 July 1998
The trackbed can still be seen, but there is little else to indicate that a small station was once located here. Passenger services over the St Boswells-Tweedmouth line ceased on 15 June 1964 and the line closed completely between Kelso and St Boswells (Kelso Junction) on 1 April 1968. *Author*

Now: 27 July 1998
The station at Roxburgh is now a fine private house with an extensive and well-kept garden. The Jedburgh branch was to close completely on 10 August 1964. Passenger services between St Boswells and Tweedmouth ceased on 15 June 1964 and the line was to close completely between St Boswells and Kelso on 1 April 1968. *Author*

Jedburgh

Then: 1950
This was the terminus of the branch from Roxburgh. It opened on 17 July 1856 and by the time of this photograph had already lost its passenger services. These had been withdrawn on 13 September 1948 as a result of serious flooding in the area and were never resumed. This is the view looking north from the buffer stops. The branch was 10 miles in length and in 1947, shortly before closure, had a service of five return trains per day.
Ian Allan Library (LGRP 24668)

Now: 27 July 1998
The line retained its freight services until 10 August 1964 when it was to close completely. As can be seen, the site has been completely redeveloped for industrial use and all traces of the railway have vanished. *Author*

Selkirk

Then: 1950
Selkirk was the terminus of a 6.25-mile long branch that joined the Waverley route at Galashiels. The line opened on 5 April 1856. The passenger service was limited by the date of this photograph; in 1947 there were two return workings per day. This view, taken in 1950, shows the branch terminus during its last days as a passenger line.
Ian Allan Library (LGRP 24660)

Kelso

Then: Undated (early 1950s)
This was one of the main stations on the North British section of the through line from St Boswells to Tweedmouth. The line opened from St Boswells to the outskirts of Kelso on 17 June 1850 and thence to Kelso (Maxwellhaugh) on 1 June 1851. The new line was but 1.5 miles from the existing North Eastern Railway line from Tweedmouth; this was soon connected and an end-on junction with the NER line was made at Sprouston Junction. Here Class V1 2-6-2T No 67659 sets back into the bay platform with the 4.5pm service from St Boswells to Kelso in order to pick up a van. *N. R. Knight*

Now: 28 July 1998
Passenger services between St Boswells and Tweedmouth ceased on 15 June 1964. The line east of Kelso to Tweedmouth was to close completely on 29 March 1965. Finally, the link between Kelso and St Boswells was to close completely on 1 April 1968. As can be seen redevelopment work was taking place at the time of my visit in mid-1998. A new road had been built with the consequent demolition of the old road bridge illustrated in the 'Then' photograph. *Author*

Now: 27 July 1998
Passenger services were withdrawn between Selkirk and Galashiels on 10 September 1951, but freight services continued to operate until 2 November 1964. Part of the station site has been redeveloped and the old railway buildings demolished, but there is still a wide open space where the railway once stood. *Author*

Galashiels

Then: 1950
An unidentified Class B1 4-6-0 prepares to depart from the station with a southbound local train. This was probably the largest station on the Waverley route and first opened for services on 20 February 1849. Its importance grew with the opening of the branch to Selkirk on 5 April 1856.
Ian Allan Library (24657)

Now: 27 July 1998
Passenger services between Edinburgh and Carlisle via Galashiels ceased on 6 January 1969 and the section between Lady Victoria Colliery and Hawick was to close completely on 28 April 1969. The station area here has been completely redeveloped, with one of the new buildings forming the local health centre. A new road has also been built. The road bridge, which spanned the station, is still extant and can just be seen in the trees. If the proposed reopening of the line to Hawick is to proceed, locations like Galashiels and Melrose, where developments have taken place which impact on the original trackbed, will have to be negotiated.
Author

Gorebridge

Then: 26 September 1964
This photograph shows BR Standard Class 4MT No 76049 departing from the station with the 12 noon Hawick-Edinburgh (Waverley) local train. By this time, this service was one of the relatively few passenger services remaining. The section of the future Waverley route from Newtongrange to Gorebridge opened on 14 July 1847; it was extended south from Gorebridge to Bowland Bridge on 4 May 1848.
W. A. C. Smith

Fountainhall

Then: 5 January 1969
This was the day before the closure of the Waverley route to passenger services as a through line. The RCTS organised a special from Leeds to Edinburgh and return. Motive power was provided in the form of 'Deltic' No D9007 *Pinza* and the train is pictured at Fountainhall Junction. Fountainhall was the junction for the short-lived Lauder Light Railway, which opened on 2 July 1901 and which closed to passenger services as long ago as 12 September 1932. The Lauder line closed completely on 1 October 1958. *Author*

Now: 27 July 1998
Despite significant local opposition, the Waverley route lost its passenger services on 6 January 1969 and this section was to close completely on 28 April of the same year. The station building here has been converted into a fine house and the trackbed remains. *Author*

Now: 28 July 1998
Passenger services through Gorebridge ceased on 6 January 1969 and the line closed completely on 28 April 1969. This was the sight that greeted me almost 30 years after closure; nothing now remained of the railway as an estate of new houses had been built on the station site — yet another barrier to potential reopening. *Author*

Eskbank & Dalkeith

Then: July 1960
One of the many 'V1' and 'V3' class 2-6-2Ts allocated to St Margarets, No 67649, is pictured arriving at Eskbank at the head of a local train from Edinburgh (Waverley) to Gorebridge. *J. C. Baker*

Now: 28 July 1998
This was the scene when I visited the site. At first the comparison appears to indicate that there is nothing left of the station, but careful examination will show that the platform on the right can still be seen, that the footbridge is still standing (but not in use) and that the stone road bridge still survives. Some 150yd behind the point from which I took the photograph, the trackbed has been converted into a cycleway and footpath. *Author*

Gullane

Then: 21 June 1958
The short branch from Aberlady Junction, on the East Coast main line, to Gullane on the south side of the Firth of Forth opened on 1 April 1898. Regular passenger services over the line ceased on 12 September 1932 and thus, by the date of this photograph, the line was freight-only with occasional excursions, as on this occasion. Gresley Class V3 No 67624 is pictured ready to leave the station with a Sunday School special. In addition to the features illustrated, there was also a small shed for the branch locomotive. *W. S. Sellar*

Now: 28 July 1998
The line was to close completely on 15 June 1964 and, after more than 30 years, the station area is now being redeveloped with a new housing estate. In the background can be seen the tower of the regional fire service training centre; this building used to be the Marine Hotel. *Author*

Edinburgh (Waverley) (east)

Then: July 1955

Class A3 No 60093 *Coronach* leaves Waverley with the up 10.5am service to London (St Pancras). This service was later named the 'Waverley'. The locomotive was allocated to Carlisle Canal shed for over 21 years and must have worked this train on many occasions. The future Waverley station first opened — as North Bridge — with the North British line from Edinburgh to Berwick on 18 June 1846; it was linked westwards to Haymarket (and the Edinburgh & Glasgow Railway) on 1 August 1846. The station was known variously as

'General' and 'Waverley Bridge', but the name 'Waverley' became generally accepted from the mid-1850s. By the later years of the 19th century, the services provided by the NBR had outgrown the cramped station initially constructed and the station, along with the lines through Princes Street Gardens, was reconstructed between 1892 and 1900. The station as illustrated here was the result of that rebuilding. *George Heiron*

Now: 7 February 1999

The skyline has altered little over the 44-year period, but, as can be seen, the trackwork has been rationalised and the East Coast main line has been electrified. The station roof and interior appear to be in much better condition. All the old goods yards and warehouses to the left have vanished, to be replaced by the inevitable car parks. A Class 305 EMU is seen on the right awaiting its next duty and an EWS/Rfd Class 90/0 is also present. The pictures were taken from the pavement where 'Jacob's Ladder' — the long stairway from below — reaches the top. Currently, Railtrack has further plans to develop the station area. *Author*

Edinburgh (Waverley) (west)

Then: 31 August 1956
Eastfield (Glasgow)-allocated Class B1 4-6-0 No 61140, fitted with self-weighing tender, approaches the west end of Waverley station with an express from Glasgow (Queen Street). The section through Princes Street Gardens, linking Haymarket with Waverley, was quadrupled during the 1890s as part of the NBR's expansion programme for Waverley station. *Author*

Now: 7 February 1999
Like the east end of the station, the trackwork at the west end of Waverley has been rationalised. The North British Hotel, at the east end of Princes Street, still dominates the skyline and little seems to have changed over the past 43 years. The view was taken from behind the Scottish National Gallery. Electrification is much less prominent at the west end of Waverley; the lines to Carstairs are electrified, thereby allowing GNER services from London (King's Cross) to run through to Glasgow (Central). *Author*

Leith (Central)

Then: Undated
The North British branch to Leith (Central) opened on 1 July 1903, although Leith itself had been rail-served by antecedents of the NBR from the mid-1830s. Passenger services to the terminus ceased on 7 April 1952 when the building was converted into a DMU maintenance depot. It was to continue in this role until closure on 29 April 1972. Following closure, the site was left derelict. *Ian Allan Library*

Now: 28 July 1998
After being derelict for almost 20 years, the remains of Leith (Central) station were demolished in 1990. The site has subsequently been redeveloped and is now occupied by the Scotmid Co-op as shown here. *Author*

Saughton Junction

Then: 8 April 1964
Class V2 No 60931, in terrible external condition, passes the junction with an eastbound coal train. The lines on the left head towards Glasgow whilst those on the right head towards the Forth Bridge. The junction was 3.5 miles west of Waverley station. *A. A. Vickers*

Joppa
Then: 10 June 1959

The original station at Joppa, which was located about four miles east of Edinburgh (Waverley), opened in 1847 and was replaced by a second station in 1859. Here a Metro-Cammell DMU (later Class 101) calls at the station on its way east with a service to North Berwick. *W. E. Turnbull*

Now: 28 July 1998
Joppa station closed on 7 September 1964 and all signs of the station platforms have long since vanished. The station building, however, can still be seen behind the bushes in the background. Note that the bridge has been modified to allow for the electrification of the line. *Author*

Now: 29 July 1998
The changes here have been dramatic. Although the lines to Glasgow and the Forth Bridge remain, there is now no junction at this point. All the sidings behind the now-demolished signalbox have disappeared, and the whole area has been tidied up. One of the Haymarket-based Class 158s, No 158709, heads north towards the Forth Bridge and the Fife circle. *Author*

St Leonards

Then: 25 August 1962
Ex-North British Class J35 0-6-0 No 64510 worked an SLS special around Edinburgh on 25 August 1962. It travelled over the St Leonards branch, which had originally opened as a horse-operated section of the Edinburgh & Dalkeith Railway on 4 July 1831. It ran to the south side of Arthur's Seat and then through a short tunnel into the yard. The train is pictured ready to depart from the terminus. The tunnel, which was on a steep gradient, was just behind me when I took this photograph. St Leonards station closed for the first time to passenger services on 1 November 1847; it reopened for a brief period, from 1 June 1860 until 30 September 1860, but was then used for goods traffic only. *Author*

Now: 29 July 1998
The line from St Leonards to the junction with the Edinburgh Suburban line at Duddingston closed completely on 5 August 1968. As can be seen, the station area has been redeveloped, but the tunnel and trackbed behind me have been converted into a cycle track and walkway. *Author*

Dalmeny Junction

Then: 20 July 1959
The junction is around half a mile south of Dalmeny station on the southern approaches to the Forth Bridge. The cantilevered bridge can be seen in the background. Carlisle Kingmoor-allocated 'Jubilee' No 45724 *Warspite*, which was obviously out of the works recently, is about to take the third side of the triangle towards Winchburgh Junction with the 3.36pm Thornton Junction-Glasgow (Queen Street) service. The appearance of a 'Jubilee' on this working was most unusual.
W. A. C. Smith

Blackford Hill

Then: 6 April 1964
This location is on the south side of Edinburgh on the Suburban circle. Here Gresley 'A3' Pacific No 60100 *Spearmint*, once one of the best kept Pacifics at Haymarket, looks in a sorry state as it approaches the site of the station with a train from Millerhill to Aberdeen (Ferryhill). The Edinburgh, Suburban & Southside Junction Railway opened on 1 December 1884 and, by the date of this photograph, passenger services over the line had ceased (on 10 September 1962). The line was retained for freight traffic bypassing Edinburgh (Waverley). *G. M. Staddon/ Neville Stead Collection*

Now: 29 July 1998
The Suburban route remains open for freight traffic and EWS-liveried Class 60 No 60024 heads west on an empty MGR working on this occasion. The crossover and third line have now been removed as has the signalbox, whilst as elsewhere the vegetation has grown considerably. *Author*

Now: 29 July 1998
Apart from track rationalisation and the inevitable growth of the vegetation, little has changed here. Class 158 No 158709 heads towards Edinburgh (Waverley) having completed a working over the Fife circle. *Author*

South Queensferry

Then: 25 March 1959
The line from Dalmeny to South Queensferry opened on 1 June 1868 and it was extended from South Queensferry to Port Edgar on 1 October 1878. The line lost much of its importance with the opening of the Forth Bridge on 4 March 1890 and passenger services were withdrawn on 14 January 1929. Freight continued thereafter, and the line was to become one of the last regular steam workings in Scotland. In its later years, the branch became associated with the now-preserved Class J36 No 65243 *Maude*, but on this occasion sister locomotive No 65258 was in charge of the service. The main line to the Forth Bridge is at a higher level to the left and the Forth Bridge can be clearly seen in the background. *W. S. Sellar*

Now: 29 July 1998
A lone walker heads towards the Firth of Forth along the pathway that now occupies the trackbed. As can be seen the road bridge in the background still exists, although the level of the trackbed has been raised slightly. The growth of the vegetation precludes a view of the Forth Bridge. The South Queensferry line was to close completely on 7 February 1966. *Author*

North Queensferry

Then: 3 July 1965
This view, taken from the station footbridge, is looking south towards the Forth Bridge. Haymarket-allocated Class B1 No 61261 approaches the station hauling the 1.10pm Edinburgh (Waverley)-Dundee stopping train. Although there had been an earlier station called North Queensferry, this station, one of two owned by the Forth Bridge Railway (as the jointly owned company controlling the Forth Bridge was called), opened with the new railway bridge on 4 March 1890. *J. A. Lockett*

Now: 27 October 1998
The station used to be well kept back in 1965, but it now appeared to be unstaffed, whilst the bushes on the platform and surrounding area have flourished, partly obscuring the view of the bridge and Firth of Forth. Class 150/2 Sprinter No 150262 approaches at 11.00 heading north for Kirkcaldy. *Author*

Inverkeithing

Then: May 1963

The line to North Queensferry from Dunfermline opened on 1 November 1877. The junction with the Forth Bridge Railway, opened on 4 March 1890, was situated just to the south of Inverkeithing station. It appears in this view that the road bridge to the north of the station was being demolished, in readiness for the road layout that still exists. An ex-NBR Class J37 0-6-0 is pictured in the station with a Rosyth Dockyard-Edinburgh train (which reverses at this point), whilst a Class 4MT 2-6-0 waits to back on to the train to take it south to its destination. *R. D. Stephen*

Now: 27 October 1998

The car park created since 1963 was almost completely full, as Inverkeithing has now become a commuter station for Edinburgh. Class 150/2 Sprinter No 150283 leaves at 10.48 heading for Markinch. The Forth Bridge can be seen on the skyline. Apart from the new car park, other changes include replacement signalling and a new station building on the down side. *Author*

Aberdour

Then: 3 April 1954
The section of line from Inverkeithing to Burntisland along the north bank of the Firth of Forth opened on 2 June 1890 following the completion of the Forth Bridge when Edinburgh services could travel direct to Fife and travellers no longer had to make use of the ferry service to Burntisland. Here Thornton-allocated Class B1 No 61103 is pictured arriving at the station with the 2.45pm semi-fast service from Thornton to Edinburgh (Waverley). *E. M. Patterson*

Now: 27 October 1998
Aberdour station remains in use although the sidings have gone and the trees have grown considerably. A frequent local service operates to and from Edinburgh and the north.
Class 150/2 No 150228 is seen leaving at 10.30 on a Fife circle working. The station has always been very well kept and has won several awards. *Author*

Dysart

Then: 26 October 1966
The station at Dysart opened with the line from Burntisland to Cupar on 20 September 1847. The picture shows Thornton-allocated 'WD' 2-8-0 No 90117 heading an up short coal train from Frances Colliery; the colliery was connected to the main line by a branch to the right (the junction is just out of the picture in the background). Class J37 No 64570 can also be seen in the background at the head of another coal train. *W. A. C. Smith*

Now: 27 October 1998
Dysart station closed on 6 October 1969 and, almost 30 years after this closure, there is now nothing to indicate that a station once existed here. One point of reference is the footbridge visible in the background. Frances Colliery, like so much of the British coal industry, is now no more; it closed in the early 1980s with its main line connection closing on 2 October 1982. *Author*

Thornton Junction

Then: 26 June 1957

Situated on the line from Burntisland to Cupar, which opened on 20 September 1847, Thornton became a junction with the opening of the lines to Crossgates (towards Dunfermline) on 4 September 1848 and to Leven on 3 July 1854. Known originally as 'Thornton', the suffix 'Junction' was added by the LNER in 1923. Fort William-allocated Class 5 No 44973 appears to be well away from its normal duties as it calls with an up local working. Whilst Thornton was a major railway centre until the demise of the Fife coalfield, the actual station structure was relatively insignificant. *Brian Morrison*

Now: 27 October 1998
Thornton Junction station closed on 6 October 1969 and, whilst the junction remains (even if the line to Methil now only carries freight), there is nothing left of the station. Fortunately, there were some Railtrack employees who were able to identify the point at which the station once stood. *Author*

Markinch

Then: September 1966
A local Class B1 4-6-0, No 61102, prepares to head south from the station after shunting in the yard with a whisky train. The station at Markinch opened with the line from Burntisland to Cupar on 20 September 1847. It was to become a junction with the opening of the short branch to Leslie in 1857.
J. M. French

Now: 27 October 1998
Very little seems to have altered during the past 32 years. The shed on the left is now out of use, but used to house the preserved Class A4 No 60009 *Union of South Africa* after the locomotive's stay on the now-closed Lochty Railway. Class 158 No 158707 calls at the station with the late-running Edinburgh (Waverley)-Dundee service at 12.55. The Leslie branch lost its passenger services on 4 January 1932 and was largely closed throughout, except for a short spur to Auchmuty, on 9 October 1967. *Author*

Cupar

Then: 1935
This view, taken looking north, shows a train departing in the Dundee direction. The line from Burntisland to Cupar opened on 20 September 1847; it was to be extended northwards to Leuchars on 17 May 1848.
Ian Allan Library (LGRP 6417)

Now: 27 October 1998
Some 63 years on, little has changed at Cupar. There has been some rationalisation of track and the goods yard has been converted into a bus and car park. On this occasion, Class 158 No 158739 is pictured arriving with the 13.50 departure to Edinburgh (Waverley). *Author*

Ladybank North Junction

Then: 5 July 1966
This station was opened by the Edinburgh & Northern Railway on 20 September 1846. Its importance grew with the opening of the lines to Hilton Junction (Perth) on 18 July 1848 and to Auchtermuchty on 6 July 1857. By the date of this photograph, passenger services over both the lines to Perth and Auchtermuchty had ceased, on 9 September 1955 and 5 June 1950 respectively, although both remained open for freight traffic. Here the line towards Dundee curves off to the right. One of the ex-NBR Class J38s, No 65919, is shunting the yard with some ballast wagons. Virtually all the 'J38s' spent their working days in the Edinburgh and Fife areas. *J. M. Boyes*

Now: 27 October 1998
The line to Auchtermuchty was to close completely on 5 October 1964. However, passenger services were restored to the Ladybank-Perth line on 6 October 1975. The signals and signalbox from the earlier view have disappeared in favour of colour lights, and the track has been rationalised. *Author*

Leuchars Junction

Then: 26 March 1954
Class 5 No 44954 appears to be allocated to Dundee Tay Bridge shed as it has a '62B' shedplate. It is occupying the bay platform at the south end of the station ready to leave with a train for St Andrews. The line from Cupar to Leuchars opened on 17 May 1848. The line was extended to Tayport, for a ferry crossing of the Tay to Dundee, on 17 May 1850. The branch to St Andrews opened on 1 July 1852. Finally, the line to Wormit opened on 30 May 1878, at which time a new station was built at Leuchars. The town's importance grew with the opening of a major RAF base and behind the locomotive can be seen some of the houses provided for RAF personnel. *Ian Allan Library*

Auchtermuchty

Then: June 1960
The line from Ladybank through Auchtermuchty to Strathmiglo opened on 6 July 1857 and thence through to Kinross in 1858. By the date of this special train, hauled by preserved ex-NBR 'Glen' 4-4-0 No 256 *Glen Douglas*, passenger services over the route had ceased — on 5 June 1950 — although the station still appeared to be in good condition despite a decade of closure. This was a joint SLS/RCTs special and the then RCTS Chairman, Bert Hurst, appears to be enjoying the pleasant day. *Ian Allan Library (K4298)*

Now: 27 October 1998
The line was closed completely between Auchtermuchty and Ladybank on 5 October 1964 and between Auchtermuchty and Mawcarse on 9 October 1967. The station is now part of the offices of the Stirling superstore, with the depot having been built along the trackbed. If one looks closely through the trees, you can see that modern offices have been erected above the original station building, which is most unusual. *Author*

Now: 27 October 1998
There are new platform lights and the bay platform has been filled in, but otherwise very little has changed in this view. Elsewhere, however, there have been significant changes. The line to Tayport lost its passenger services (and closed completely) on 9 January 1956; a short stub — recently closed — was retained to serve the airfield. Passenger services on the St Andrews branch followed on 6 January 1969, at which time it was to close completely. Here Class 158 No 158746 is pictured in the station ready to leave with the 15.42 service to Edinburgh (Waverley). *Author*

Kilmany

Then: 2 June 1950
This was one of three intermediate stations on the North Fife line from St Fort to Newburgh (Glenburnie Junction). This delightful picture shows ex-CR 0-4-4T No 55213 heading the 6.8pm Dundee-Perth train. The line opened on 25 January 1909. *E. M. Patterson*

Now: 27 October 1998
Despite local opposition which forced a delay to the planned closure, the line lost its passenger services on 12 February 1951. The line closed completely between St Fort and Lindores, including Kilmany, on 5 October 1964. The westernmost section of the route, from Lindores to Glenburnie Junction, closed earlier, on 4 April 1960. The location was difficult to find, mainly because there was nobody about to give advice. My thanks are due to the lady in one of the houses, who I got out of her sick bed to get permission to take the photograph from her garden. The station site has been converted into a small development of some four pleasant houses. *Author*

Leven

Then: Undated (c1950s)

Leven was the junction for the two lines which headed inland towards Thornton Junction, one via Methil and one via Cameron Bridge. The railway first reached Leven on 3 July 1854. The line was extended along the Fife coast to Kilconquhar on 8 July 1857 at which time a new station was built in the town. *E. M. Patterson*

Now: 27 October 1998

Passenger services north of Leven ceased on 6 September 1965 and the line was to close completely north of the town on 18 July 1966. Passenger services between Thornton and Leven via Methil ceased on 10 January 1955 and the line closed completely south of Methil on 15 October 1966. Finally, passenger services between Thornton and Leven via Cameron Bridge were withdrawn on 6 October 1969. The line remains open from Thornton to Methil, although, as can be seen, nothing now remains at this location to indicate that a railway once existed here other than the name Station Court on the houses and the Station Hotel which is located nearby. *Author*

Elie

Then: Undated (mid-1960s)
Elie is a pleasant holiday town on the Fife coast. The station opened, with the line from Leven to Kilconquhar, on 8 July 1857. The line was largely single track with passing loops as here. *J. Mackay*

Now: 27 October 1998
The line between Leven and St Andrews lost its passenger services on 6 September 1965 and was to close completely south of Crail on 18 July 1966. The entire site at Elie has now been redeveloped for housing and the only sign of the railway was the old footbridge from which I took this photograph. I am sure that, had the line survived the closures of the 1960s, it would have prospered today as the number of visitors to the coast has increased dramatically over the years and St Andrews is a hugely popular town — not just for the golf. *Author*

Gordoun

Then: 22 April 1962
This was the penultimate station on the branch which ran along the coast of Kincardineshire from Broomfield Junction, Montrose, to Inverbervie. The line was opened throughout on 1 November 1865 and, by the date of this photograph, normal passenger services had been withdrawn (on 1 October 1951). Here a railtour heads southbound back towards Montrose behind Type 1 (later Class 20) No D8028. *W. S. Sellar*

Kilconquhar

Then: Undated (mid-1960s)
This was one of the many intermediate stations on the Fife Coast line from Leven to St Andrews. The line opened from Leven to Kilconquhar on 8 July 1857. It was extended from here to Anstruther on 1 September 1863. As can be seen, the station boasted but a single platform and, given the state of the track, it is possible that this photograph (and that at Elie) portrays the line shortly after closure. *J. Mackay*

Now: 27 October 1998
It was extremely difficult to find the exact location, but I believe that the gate shown was in the same place as the level crossing gates; apart from the trackbed there was nothing to indicate that the station ever existed. Passenger services north of Leven to St Andrews ceased on 6 September 1965 and the line closed completely between Crail and Leven on 18 July 1966. *Author*

Now: 27 May 1998
The same view, taken 36 years later shows how little has changed at this location other than the disappearance of the railway line and the alteration to the breakwater. The line to Inverbervie was to close completely on 23 May 1966. *Author*

Inverbervie

Then: 13 July 1961
Called 'Bervie' when first opened on 1 November 1865, the station was renamed 'Inverbervie' on 5 July 1926. The line from Broomfield Junction at Montrose was some 13 miles long and in 1947, some four years before the withdrawal of passenger services (on 1 October 1951), the line could claim three return workings per day. On this occasion, the daily freight to Montrose was being hauled by Class J37 No 64598, which is pictured ready to start on its return journey. *M. Pope*

Now: 27 May 1998
The freight service to Inverbervie lasted until 23 May 1966 when the line closed completely. The whole area has been subsequently landscaped and no traces of the station area remain. *Author*

Alloa

Then: 22 August 1966
Alloa was served by both the North British and Caledonian railways. This is the ex-NBR station. The NBR first reached Alloa from Oakley, to the east, on 28 August 1850 and the town developed into a significant junction with NBR lines radiating to Tillicoultry (opened 3 June 1851), to Stirling (opened 1 July 1852) and

Kincardine (opened 18 December 1893), as well as the ex-CR route to Alloa Junction (which opened on 1 October 1885). The NBR station was known as Alloa North from 1882. Here BR Standard Class 4MT No 76109 negotiates the junction with a Dollar Colliery-Alloa freight. *P. R. Parham*

Now: 25 October 1998
There has been considerable change at Alloa over the years. All the lines which served Alloa have lost their passenger services; the last to succumb were those from Oakley to Stirling, which ceased on 7 October 1968. A number of the lines have also closed completely; the line through Tillicoultry to Dollar closed on 25 June 1973 — this line was initially viewed by the Scottish Railway Preservation Society as an option for preservation — whilst the ex-CR route had succumbed (from Alloa West Junction to Longcarse Junction) on 18 May 1970. The line towards Oakley closed on 6 October 1979, leaving the line from Stirling to Kincardine and Dunfermline operational. The section through Alloa is now disused, although the track is still evident (but covered in undergrowth) in this view. There has been talk for a number of years of the possibility of reopening the line from Stirling to Dunfermline via Alloa to passenger and freight services. Beyond the bridge, a factory has been built on part of the former railway land. *Author*

Alva

Then: June 1962
A joint RCTS/SLS Scottish railtour visited the branch terminus at Alva in June 1962 and here the locomotive is pictured running round its train. Alva was the terminus of a 5.5-mile-long branch which left the Stirling-Alloa line at Cambus. The line opened on 3 June 1863 and, by the date of this excursion had already closed to passenger services on 1 November 1954.
Ian Allan Library (K5141)

Now: 25 October 1998
Freight services over the branch beyond the one intermediate station at Menstrie ceased on 2 March 1964. As can be seen, the station building at Alva remains some 34 years after complete closure, although the surrounding area has altered dramatically. *Author*

Dunfermline (Lower)

Then: 1 August 1953
There was a veritable network of ex-NBR lines serving Dunfermline and district. Dunfermline (Lower) — it was retitled simply 'Dunfermline' by BR later — is situated on the line from Inverkeithing to Crossgates, which opened from Dunfermline to North Queensferry on 1 November 1877. The importance of the line grew considerably with the opening of the Forth Bridge in March 1890. Here Gresley Class V3 2-6-2T No 67672, allocated to Dunfermline shed, prepares to leave with a local train for Edinburgh (Waverley). *Brian Morrison*

Dollar

Then: 14 July 1955
One of the ex-North British Railway Class D34 'Glens', No 62470 *Glen Roy*, pauses at the station at the head of the 2.45pm train from Stirling to Perth via the Devon Valley line. The Devon Valley line opened from Alloa to Tillicoultry on 3 June 1851 and thence to Dollar on 3 May 1869. The line was extended northwards from Dollar to Rumbling Bridge, where it connected with a line from Kinross, on 1 May 1871. *W. A. Camwell*

Now: 25 October 1998
Passenger services over the Alloa-Kinross via Dollar line ceased on 15 June 1964 at which time the line closed completely between Dollar and Kinross. The section south of Dollar remained open for freight, largely to serve a colliery in Dollar, until complete closure on 25 June 1973. As can be seen, although the trackbed and platform edging survive at the station, little else remains to remind people that this was once a railway station. *Author*

Now: 27 October 1998
The station buildings on the down side remain virtually unaltered, but the up platform has been reduced to a small waiting room. The old wooden platform has been replaced. Haymarket Class 158 No 158716 prepares to leave for Edinburgh (Waverley) at 11.33. The unit was probably doing a filling-in turn on the Fife circle between Aberdeen and Inverness duties. *Author*

Gartness

Then: 1935
This station was situated on the North British line from Stirling to Balloch. Slightly to the north of Gartness was the junction — Gartness Junction — with the line south to Kirkintilloch. This picture was taken in 1935, shortly after the station had lost its passenger services — on 1 October 1934 — although the route remained open for freight traffic. The line opened from Stirling to Buchlyvie on 18 March 1856 and thence, via Gartness, to Balloch on 26 May 1856.
Ian Allan Library (LGRP 6416)

Now: 21 October 1998
The section of line from Dryman — the next station along the line towards Balloch — and Gartness Junction closed completely on 1 November 1950. Today the road bridge over the track — behind the photographer — is still extant and the trackbed can still be identified as it heads west. Under the bridge there are still signs of the platform, but otherwise the site has returned to nature. To the right is a well-patronised cafe. *Author*

Lennoxtown

Then: 28 May 1949
Ex-North British Class D34 4-4-0 No 62497 *Glen Mallie* is in the station on a passenger working. The 5.5-mile-long line from Lenzie Junction, to the south of Kirkintilloch, to Lennoxtown opened on 5 July 1848. The line was extended northwards, courtesy of the Blane Valley Railway, to Killearn for freight on 5 November 1866 and to passengers on 1 July 1867.
G. H. Robin

Strathblane

Then: 1935
This was one of a number of intermediate stations between Gartness Junction and Kirkintilloch on the line which ran to the south of the Campsie Fells. This view is taken looking south towards Campsie. The Blane Valley line from Lennoxtown through Strathblane to Killearn opened for freight on 5 November 1866 and to passenger traffic on 1 July 1867; it was later extended from Killearn, via Gartness Junction, to Aberfoyle. At this date, 1935, the line was still served by both passenger and freight trains.
Ian Allan Library (LGRP 6413)

Now: 21 October 1998
Passengers over the line from Kirkintilloch to Aberfoyle via Strathblane ceased on 1 October 1951 and the line closed completely north of Lennoxtown on 5 October 1959. The railway embankment to the road bridge situated behind me still exists but, as can be seen, the station area has been landscaped. The station house is to the left of the picture. *Author*

Now: 21 October 1998
Passenger services from Kirkintilloch to Aberfoyle ceased on 1 October 1951 and the line north of Lennox Castle Hospital Siding closed completely on 5 October 1959. The short section from Lennoxtown to the siding at the hospital ceased on 28 September 1964 and, finally, the line south to Lenzie Junction closed completely on 4 April 1966. The flooded football pitch gives a fair indication of the weather in the area on this occasion. Apart from the road bridge on which I was standing to take the picture, all traces of the railway have vanished. *Author*

Kirkintilloch

Then: 28 October 1961

This excellent picture — showing the station looking north towards the Campsie Fells — shows clean Austerity 2-8-0 No 90128 heading a down freight from Kilsyth past English Electric Type 1 (later Class 20) No D8082. The station opened with the line from Lenzie Junction, on the Edinburgh-Glasgow main line — to Lennoxtown on 5 July 1848; the new station replaced an earlier station called Kirkintilloch on the Edinburgh & Glasgow Railway main line. These lines were not the first to serve Kirkintilloch, however, as the Monklands & Kirkintilloch opened in 1826 to provide a link to the Forth & Clyde Canal at Kirkintilloch; this was the first railway to be authorised to use locomotives, although steam was not actually introduced until the early 1830s. Just north of Kirkintilloch there was a spur that linked the line towards Lennoxtown into the line towards Kilsyth. Passenger services to Aberfoyle had already ceased by the date of this photograph — on 1 October 1951 — although it remained open to freight as far as Lennoxtown. *S. Rickard*

Now: 21 October 1998

Passenger services from Lenzie Junction to Kirkintilloch ceased on 7 September 1964 and the line from Lenzie Junction to Lennoxtown closed completely on 4 April 1966. Today, it is really very hard to believe that this is the same location. All traces of the railway — and the adjacent foundry — have gone. The connecting feature between the two photographs is the tower/spire in the distance; this building is now a tandoori restaurant. The picture was taken from the towpath of the Forth & Clyde Canal. The weather was so bad when I took this picture that the Campsie Fells could not be seen in the distance. *Author*

Bo'ness

Then: 12 July 1955
One of the four ex-CR Class 431 0-4-4Ts, which were a development of the earlier Class 439 locomotives, No 55238, is ready to leave the station on the 5.22pm working to Polmont, whilst ex-NBR Class J36 0-6-0 No 65275 awaits its next shunting duties. Bo'ness — short for Borrowstounness — was one of the harbours on the Forth; it suffered significantly from the rise of the neighbouring Grangemouth (to the west) and was also a location where CR and NBR rivalry was to the fore. The line to Bo'ness was built under the auspices of the Slammannan & Borrowstounness Railway and opened on 17 March 1851. Although an NBR line eventually, rivalry with the CR was reflected in the fact that a service operated by the CR to Glasgow (Buchanan Street) operated for some months in 1899. *W. A. Camwell*

Now: 29 July 1998
Passenger services ceased to Bo'ness on 7 May 1956, whilst freight facilities were withdrawn on 7 June 1965. The line remained open to Kinneil, to serve the colliery, until 16 July 1979. I needed the help of several local people before I could get this picture sorted out as the changes have been dramatic. The link between the two pictures is the tall building to the far left. The area has been extensively landscaped and, as can be seen, nothing now remains to indicate the presence of the railway. The new station of the preserved Bo'ness & Kinneil Railway — run by the Scottish Railway Preservation Society — is about half a mile to the east. *Author*

Bathgate shed

Then: 6 February 1955

This picture of the rather ugly modern shed at Bathgate was taken on 6 February 1955 and shows a selection of ex-NBR Class J36 0-6-0s, along with an 'N15' and a 'B1'. The shed was used primarily to house locomotives required for use on the many freight services around Bathgate, in particular traffic to and from the local collieries.

In the early 1960s, Bathgate became a dump for withdrawn locomotives, with many of the fine Haymarket-allocated Pacifics spending some time here. The original six-road shed at Bathgate, which was coded '64F' by BR, was rebuilt in 1954 to the structure illustrated here as a result of subsidence damage. *Author*

Now: 29 July 1998

The shed closed in 1966 but is still in existence. The building is now used to house a vehicle repair centre and can be seen behind the bushes in this view. *Author*

Airdrie

Then: 24 April 1961
Class J38 0-6-0 No 65911 heads through Airdrie at the head of a coal train for Bathgate. The Bathgate & Coatbridge Railway, via Airdrie, opened on 11 August 1862, thereby providing a further direct link between Edinburgh and Glasgow as the earlier Edinburgh &

Bathgate Railway had opened on 12 November 1849. In this picture the sidings adjacent to the station can be seen, whilst the line to the left headed into an old foundry. *W. S. Sellar*

Now: 22 October 1998
This view is taken from the road bridge to the east of the station and shows Strathclyde Class 303 EMU No 303008 arriving from Drumgelloch, to the east, with the 09.23 service to Glasgow. The whole area has been redeveloped, with a new road on the right and a shopping complex to the left. Passenger services to the east of Airdrie via Bathgate to Edinburgh ceased on 9 January 1956, although electrified services were extended to Drumgelloch on 15 May 1989. The Airdrie line was electrified on 5 November 1960 and the station has been rebuilt. The line between Airdrie and Bathgate remained for freight traffic until the early 1980s, when it was severed to the east of Plains on 1 February 1982. *Author*

Cowlairs Bank

Then: 13 July 1956
Eastfield-allocated Stanier Class 5 No 44908 gets help from a banker as it climbs the 1 in 41 bank out of Glasgow (Queen Street) at the head of the 10.15am service to Mallaig. Pinkston Power Station can just be seen behind the exhaust of the locomotive; this supplied electricity to Glasgow Corporation for the latter's tram, trolleybus and Underground systems. The line to Queen Street station opened on 21 February 1842 under the auspices of the Edinburgh & Glasgow Railway; when the line first opened, such was the gradient that trains to and from the terminus used ropes and it was not until November 1908 that conventional motive power replaced beam engines and rope haulage over the incline. *Author*

Now: 21 October 1998
This view was taken from the road bridge to show more of the area. Class 158 Sprinter No 158728 climbs the gradient without any difficulty. The lines at this point are now bi-directional. The area has improved considerably over the past 40 years, with high-rise flats replacing the old tenement blocks. Pinkston Power Station has been demolished. *Author*

Glasgow (Queen Street) (High)

Then: September 1954
In steam days, Glasgow (Queen Street), both High and Low Level, was a gloomy place, but extremely atmospheric if your photographic techniques were good enough to take advantage of the surroundings. In September 1954, a couple of Eastfield-allocated Class 5s make a vigorous departure at the head of the 3.46pm service to Fort William and Mallaig, before plunging into the darkness of the tunnel and the 1 in 41 gradient to Cowlairs station. A banking locomotive, usually a

Class N15 0-6-2T, would be working hard at the rear. To the left is a Class B1 4-6-0 at the head of what would have been the 4pm departure to Edinburgh (Waverley). The future High Level station opened on 21 February 1842; until November 1908 all arrivals and departures were worked into the station by rope. The Low Level platforms opened 44 years later. Note the fine signal gantry at the platform end. *Author*

Now: 28 October 1998
The platform from which the Mallaig train was departing in 1954 is now no more and the station at the tunnel end appears to be vanishing beneath new office blocks. Today, atmosphere is virtually non-existent, with the Sprinters, which operate all the services, arriving and departing with little effort. Class 158 No 158746 enters the tunnel with the 11.55 departure for Inverness. Cowlairs Bank is now signalled for bi-directional working. *Author*

Eastfield shed
(north end — steam)

Then: 12 July 1956
This photograph, taken on a Sunday, shows at least nine different classes of locomotive. At this time, in the mid-1950s, there would have been around 150 locomotives on shed; Polmadie would have had about 160. This view was taken from the long-dismantled bridge which crossed the shed and the main line at the north end of the site. This bridge carried the Caledonian line which ran from Maryhill via Possil to Robroyston. The shed, coded '65A' by BR, was opened by the NBR in 1904. *Author*

Now: 21 October 1998
The shed became a diesel depot in 1966 and was to close in 1992. In order to mark its closure, a Class 26 was named after the depot. The depot's allocation transferred to Motherwell on closure, which, as a result, became the main diesel depot for Scotland. The site was cleared and is now used as a permanent way store, although the old fuel tanks are still extant. The picture was taken from the west side of the main line, which is to the right of the picture, with a telephoto lens as there was no way that the original photograph could be replicated exactly. The background is now dominated by high-rise flats. *Author*

Bridgeton Central

Then: 30 August 1962
When opened on 1 June 1892, the station, the terminus of a one-mile branch from High Street on the Glasgow (Queen Street) (Low Level)-Bellhouse line, was known as Bridgeton Cross. It became Bridgeton Central in January 1954. Apart from the passenger service to the platforms shown in this view, Bridgeton was also the location of the main cleaning and washing point for the Glasgow 'Blue Trains' operating north of the river until Yoker replaced it. Several EMUs are seen parked in the sidings waiting to go through the washing plant. *S. Rickard*

Eastfield shed
(north end — diesel)

Then: 24 May 1991
This is the most recent of the 'Then' photographs in the book and is included to provide a contrast with the locomotive scene of more than 40 years ago. Shortly before complete closure, this was the scene at Eastfield; it is possible, even with the much reduced fleet of BR diesels, to see representatives of five different classes — '08', '20', '26', '37' and '47' — in a number of different liveries. *Author*

Now: 21 October 1998
The sad decline of a once great depot: Eastfield closed in 1992 and today the site has been cleared and replaced by a permanent way store. *Author*

Now: 22 October 1998
The Bridgeton Central branch lost its passenger services on 5 November 1979 and was to close completely by mid-1987 when the depot closed. The station area has been completely transformed and new houses have been built on the site. *Author*

Bishopbriggs

Then: 26 July 1955
This station is situated about three miles out of Glasgow on the Edinburgh & Glasgow Railway route which opened on 21 February 1842. It was one of 10 intermediate stations on the original line. A Perth-Glasgow (Queen Street) local service is pictured calling at the station headed by Class D11 'Director' 4-4-0 No 62686 *The Fiery Cross*, which was allocated to Eastfield. *G. H. Robin*

Now: 21 October 1998
The Edinburgh-Glasgow main line remains open, as does Bishopbriggs station. As can be seen, however, the station buildings have disappeared and the footbridge has been replaced. Class 158 No 158742 calls at the station with an evening commuter service for Glasgow (Queen Street) at 16.54. *Author*

Anniesland

Then: 11 August 1960
Gresley Class V1 2-6-2T No 67616 enters the station with a train for Bridgeton Cross. When the station and line opened on 20 October 1874 the station was called 'Great Western Road'; it was renamed 'Anniesland' on 9 January 1931. In the background can be seen the bridge carrying the line towards Helensburgh and on to Fort William. A spur headed northwest from Anniesland to connect with this line at Knightswood North Junction. The signalbox controlled the junction with this spur and the line heading northeastwards towards Maryhill; this line had lost its passenger services on 15 September 1959 and so, by this date, was freight only. As can be seen, sidings were provided on both up and down sides at this location. *Author*

Now: 21 October 1998
Class 314 No 314209 enters the station on a Dalmuir-Motherwell service as one of the original Class 303 EMUs, No 303001, leaves for Balloch. All the sidings have gone, although the gasometers survive. The line from Anniesland towards Maryhill closed completely on 14 October 1980. *Author*

Hyndland

Then: 11 August 1960
Three months before the introduction of the 'Blue Trains', a number of new units are stabled outside new depot at Hyndland. Alongside the old order, in the form of 'V1' 2-6-2T No 67605, is ready to depart. The Hyndland branch was less than one mile in length and opened on 15 March 1886. *Author*

Now: 21 October 1998
Passenger services over the Hyndland branch ceased on 5 November 1960 when a new station with the same name was opened on the main line. Thereafter, the line remained open to serve the EMU depot at Hyndland until complete closure came by mid-1987 when Yoker depot took on the maintenance of those units previously based at Hyndland. The change has been dramatic in the decade since closure. As can be seen, the site was being redeveloped into housing, with what appeared to be expensive flats under construction. All traces of the railway have disappeared; the reference point is the church tower. *Author*

Milngavie

Then: 23 July 1959
The branch to Milngavie was opened on 28 August 1863 by the Glasgow & Milngavie Junction Railway. Leaving the main line to Helensburgh via Singer at Milngavie Junction, just outside Westerton station, the branch runs for 3.25 miles and is provided with two intermediate stations (Bearsden and Hillfoot). On this occasion Gresley Class V1 2-6-2T No 67676 is pictured preparing to depart with an evening train for either Bridgeton or Airdrie. Wagons can be seen in the goods yard to the right. *Author*

Jordanhill

Then: 11 August 1960
Class V3 2-6-2T No 67627 calls at the station with a train for Airdrie. The external condition of the locomotive reflects the fact that there were only another three months to go before the introduction of the 'Blue Train' EMUs and the consequent demise of these locomotives. In the early 1950s, most of the 'V1' and 'V3' tanks used on these services were kept in an immaculate condition. Jordanhill was the centre of a triangle of lines, although only the south side was provided with platforms. The station opened on 1 August 1887. *Author*

Now: 21 October 1998
The station remains open and Class 320 EMU No 320313, in the new Strathclyde livery, calls at the station with an eastbound service for Airdrie. The fine old gas lamps seen in the 'Then' photograph have been replaced by modern lamps and the original station buildings have disappeared. *Author*

Now: 21 October 1998
The goods yard closed on 6 September 1965. The Milngavie branch was electrified on 5 November 1960 and currently the station is well kept. It has been awarded several prizes in recent years. A frequent service is provided for the many commuters in the area. The station has a large car park, for which no charge is made. Class 320 No 320304 is seen ready to leave with the 12.52 service to Springburn. *Author*

Dumbarton/Dalreoch

Then: 12 May 1960

This location is between Dumbarton and Dalreoch on the Dumbarton & Balloch Joint Line Committee — CR and NBR — route which ran for six miles. The Committee came into effect with the opening of the Lanarkshire & Dumbartonshire Railway from Clydebank to Dumbarton East; the original line, as part of the Glasgow, Dumbarton & Helensburgh Railway, had opened on 28 May 1858. The branch to Balloch headed north at a junction at Dalreoch,

slightly to the west of this point. This is the bridge over the River Leven and on this occasion, preserved ex-CR No 123 pilots ex-NBR No 256 *Glen Douglas* are on a special which was heading to Oban. As can be seen, the line had already been electrified; these services were inaugurated on 5 November 1960 but work had been in progress converting the lines north of the River Clyde since 1957. *Author*

Now: 23 October 1998

During the 38 years since the 'Then' picture was taken, three large trees have grown, partly obscuring the view of the bridge. Two of

Strathclyde's Class 320/3 EMUs, in the latest livery, head westwards on a working towards Helensburgh. *Author*

Craigendoran

Then: 11 August 1960
There were two levels to this station. The lower one is on the line to Helensburgh, opened on 15 May 1882, whilst the upper level served the West Highland line and opened on 7 August 1894. The signal seen on the top right of the photograph marks the West Highland line. In sharp contrast to the condition in which the Class V1 and V3 2-6-2Ts used to be kept on the line in the 1950s, Class V1 No 67613 enters the station from Helensburgh looking in an extremely neglected condition. *Author*

Now: 23 October 1998
The West Highland line platforms closed on 14 June 1964, but the lower level continues in use. The junction for the West Highland line is to the east of the station. The track to Helensburgh has now been singled from the junction and there is no access to the old down platform. Strathclyde Class 320 No 320301 has just arrived from Helensburgh heading east. The station is extremely run down; I believe that the buildings on the up side were destroyed by fire. *Author*

Helensburgh shed

Then: 11 August 1960
The shed had the code '65H' in its later years and had a small allocation of 'V1s' and 'V3s' for working the services to Glasgow and beyond. In the early 1950s, the locomotives were kept in immaculate condition; this is in sharp contrasts to No 67622 and another member of the class, which are recorded in terrible condition outside the shed on this occasion. This was during the period when steam was brought back to these services following the temporary withdrawal of the 'Blue Train' EMUs (the later Class 303s). The Helensburgh line — under the auspices of the Glasgow, Dumbarton & Helensburgh Railway — opened on 28 May 1858. *Author*

Now: 23 October 1998
It is now difficult to believe that a shed — which closed in 1962 — once stood on the site. Fortunately, it was possible to identify the location by the tower in the background. *Author*

Garelochhead

Then: 12 May 1962
Two of the Scottish preserved locomotives, ex-CR Single No 123 and ex-NBR No 256 *Glen Douglas*, depart from the station heading for the steep six-mile climb to the summit just before the Glen Douglas passing loop. The special was heading for Oban and would return via the Callander & Oban line. The station, like others on the section from Helensburgh to Fort William, opened on 7 August 1894. *Author*

Now: 23 October 1998
The siding on the up line has now gone, but that on the down side still exists. The trees around the station, like so many places on the line, have grown and now obscure the fine views. Like other stations on the line, Garelochhead is now unstaffed. *Author*

Arrochar & Tarbert

Then: 13 August 1960
The 10.15am from Glasgow (Queen Street) to Fort William pauses at the station on its way north. North British-built Class B1 4-6-0 No 61396 pilots BR Standard Class 5MT No 73077, both locomotives being allocated to Eastfield. The train was waiting to pass the 6.38am from Mallaig, which was headed by two Stanier Class 5s. The station, which opened on 7 August 1894, had some well tended gardens at this time. *Author*

Now: 23 October 1998
The signals have gone, as a result of the introduction of RETB, and new lighting has been installed at this now unstaffed station. Freight facilities were withdrawn on 1 November 1966 but 32 years later the sidings to the south of the station are again being used to load timber. *Author*

Ardlui

Then: 1950
This picture shows the water column on the down line, where locomotives could replenish their tenders before facing the gruelling 8.5-mile climb, mainly at 1 in 60, up the gradient through Glen Falloch. The coach dumped in the up siding would appear to have been detached from a train. The station opened on 7 August 1894. *Ian Allan Library (LGRP 24583)*

Now: 23 October 1998
Little appears to have changed over the past half-century; as is the case with many of the stations on the West Highland line. The water column has disappeared, the station building has been demolished and the signs have changed or been moved, but otherwise Ardlui is remarkably timeless. *Author*

Crianlarich Upper (south)

Then: 12 May 1962
This photograph was taken about half a mile south of Crianlarich Upper. The train is headed by two of the Scottish preserved locomotives, the ex-CR Single No 123 and ex-NBR No 256 *Glen Douglas*, and is making for Oban. From Crianlarich, the train took the spur down to the ex-CR route towards Oban and would later return via Callander. It was a magnificent day and the locomotives looked superb in their colourful liveries. The NBR line through Crianlarich opened on 7 August 1894; the connecting spur to the C&O followed on 20 December 1897. The spur was not heavily used until the closure of the C&O east of Crianlarich on 1 November 1965. *Author*

Now: 23 October 1998
As one drives around Scotland these days, one can't help but notice the vast areas of the countryside covered by fir trees. This is the case on the east side of the line just south of Crianlarich Upper. The railway is on the other side of the trees; in fact, where I stood to take the 'Then' picture was in the middle of the trees and so I had to stand back a bit in order to get this view. *Author*

Crianlarich Upper

Then: 18 June 1960
The last working of a Class K4 2-6-0 in BR service on the West Highland line occurred on 18 June 1960 when No 61995 *Cameron of Lochiel* hauled the 'White Cockade' special. The locomotive is taking water at Crianlarich Upper, whilst passengers record the event in the evening sunlight. The station opened on 7 August 1894 and was, with its connection to the C&O line to Oban, one of the more important locations on the West Highland line. The engine shed, which was a sub-shed of Eastfield, can be seen on the right of the photograph. *Author*

Now: 23 October 1998
The old shed is still in use by Railtrack and the yard is now once again in use for freight. Class 37/4 No 37410 *Aluminium 100* is at the head of a timber train and is awaiting a crew. The track layout is largely the same, but the buildings nearest the camera are new, the originals having been destroyed by fire. The others, which house the excellent cafe, are original. *Author*

Tyndrum Upper

Then: 1913
Originally called just 'Tyndrum', the station acquired the 'Upper' suffix on 21 September 1953 in order to differentiate it from 'Lower' on the line towards Oban. A number of passengers in the train are clearly fascinated by the fact that somebody wished to take a photograph of the station. The station opened on 7 August 1894.
Ian Allan Library (LGRP 7023)

Now: 23 October 1998
The station, despite being unstaffed for a number of years, has survived remarkably well. Apart from the inevitable trees which have grown on the embankment and a few bushes on the platform, the scene is largely unchanged. *Author*

Spean Bridge (east)

Then: 1905
This was the junction station for the Invergarry & Fort Augustus Railway. This line, which opened throughout on 22 July 1903 was initially operated by the Highland Railway, which was afraid that the NBR would use the line as a means of gaining access eventually to Inverness. HR trains operated until 1908 when they were replaced by NBR services; these themselves were withdrawn between 1911 and 1913. Thus, at the time of this photograph, both NBR and HR trains would have been seen at this location.
Ian Allan Library (28042)

Roy Bridge

Then: 1914
This view, taken looking west towards
Spean Bridge and Fort William, shows
the station at Roy Bridge some 20 years
after its opening on 7 August 1894. It
shows well the two platforms, the
station buildings, the signalbox and the
sidings at the west end.
Ian Allan Library

Now: 24 October 1998
It was raining so hard that I had to take
this photograph from inside the car from
the overbridge at the east end of the
station. The line has been singled and
the platform buildings replaced. The
disused up platform remains intact but
increasingly buried in vegetation. *Author*

Now: 24 October 1998
The buildings on the down side have
vanished and modern lighting has now
been installed. The rather ugly
signalbox, still stands although it has
been used as a greenhouse for a number
of years. The station buildings on the up
platform are currently in excellent order,
having been converted into a restaurant.
Author

Spean Bridge (west)

Then: 1914
This view taken looking towards Fort William shows, on the left, the lines for Fort William whilst on the right the Invergarry & Fort Augustus Railway heads off north towards its destination. The line through Spean Bridge opened on 7 August 1894 and the station became a junction with the opening of the line to Fort Augustus on 22 July 1903. *Ian Allan Library (LGRP 8290)*

Now: 24 October 1998
Never successful, the Fort Augustus line lost its passenger services on 1 December 1933 and was to close completely on 31 December 1946. Note that the platform curve at the west end still curves to allow for the former alignment. A road has replaced the trackbed into the bay once occupied by Fort Augustus trains. *Author*

Aberchalder

Then: 1914
This station, situated a few miles south of the terminus at Fort Augustus, was one of four intermediate stations between Spean Bridge and Fort Augustus. The line opened on 22 July 1903, when it was operated by the Highland Railway. The North British took over in 1908. This photograph is taken shortly after the NBR had reintroduced services; these had been suspended between 1 November 1911 and 1 August 1913. *Ian Allan Library (LGRP 8300)*

Now: 24 October 1998
Never a resounding commercial success, the Fort Augustus line lost its passenger services for the final time on 1 December 1933 and was to close completely on 31 December 1946. Some 50 years after this closure, there were still signs of the platform and the bridge still existed, albeit well hidden by the undergrowth. *Author*

Fort William (south end)

Then: 18 June 1960
This was the last working in BR service of a Gresley Class K4 to Fort William. No 61995 *Cameron of Lochiel* provided the motive power for the 'White Cockade' special from Glasgow. It is pictured at the south end of the station after arrival with one of the two local Class J36 0-6-0s ready to remove the empty stock. The picture was taken from the jetty, at which the MacBrayne buses used to park before setting off to their destinations. The line opened to Fort William from Helensburgh on 7 August 1894. The West Highland line was opened from Fort William to Banavie on 1 June 1895. *Author*

Now: 25 October 1998
The station at Fort William was relocated closer to the junction on 2 June 1975. As can be seen, the old station has been completely demolished, although the jetty still survives — now occupied by a restaurant — and a new dual carriageway has been built on the old railway formation. *Author*

Fort William (north end — looking south)

Then: 10 August 1960
A second comparison is provided at this location and the 'Then' photograph shows Class B1 No 61243 *Sir Harold Mitchell* ready to leave with a service for Glasgow (Queen Street). Alongside is local Class K1 No 62011 waiting to depart with a train to Mallaig. *Author*

Fort William
(north end — looking north)

Then: 1 September 1958
Class K2 2-6-0 No 61787 *Loch Quioch*
approaches the old station off the single
line section with a train from Mallaig.
Author

Now: 25 October 1998
The changes at Fort William have been
dramatic. The trackbed and all the old
station area have been rebuilt into this
dual carriageway. No signs of the old
station survive. The new station is
located about half-a-mile to the north.
Author

Now: 25 October 1998
The new road sweeps alongside the east
bank of Loch Linnhe avoiding the town
centre. *Author*

Fort William (shed)

Then: 1 June 1963
This view was taken on the day which saw the last train operated with BR steam power over the West Highland lines. It shows North British Type 2 No D6137, which had been sent out to rescue the failed train. The 'J37' on the left, No 64632, had run hot at Rannoch and had been removed from the train, leaving preserved No 256 *Glen Douglas* to continue alone. The latter locomotive also later failed. In the background can be seen the peak of Ben Nevis; it was a glorious summer's day, but there was still snow on the mountain's summit. *Author*

Now: 25 October 1998
Some of the land close to the shed has been redeveloped, but part was still derelict on this occasion. The view of Ben Nevis — still with snow — is still uninterrupted. *Author*

Banavie

Then: 1 June 1963
The 'Jacobite' rail tour ran on this date and marked the end of BR steam operation over the West Highland line. The train did not operate without difficulty, as both locomotives failed on the journey to Fort William and one of the Class J37s seen here crossing the swing bridge over the Caledonian Canal at Banavie ran hot during the journey and could not return. As a result, the special returned hours late behind a Type 2. The two Class J37s utilised were Nos 64592 and 64636. The line opened from Fort William to Banavie Pier on 1 June 1895 and was extended from Banavie to Mallaig on 1 April 1901. The short original line between Banavie and Banavie Pier lost its passenger services on 4 October 1939 and was to close completely on 6 August 1951. *Author*

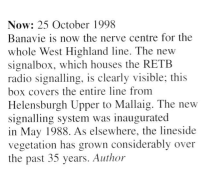

Now: 25 October 1998
Banavie is now the nerve centre for the whole West Highland line. The new signalbox, which houses the RETB radio signalling, is clearly visible; this box covers the entire line from Helensburgh Upper to Mallaig. The new signalling system was inaugurated in May 1988. As elsewhere, the lineside vegetation has grown considerably over the past 35 years. *Author*

Corpach

Then: 1913
This view, taken looking east towards Mallaig, dates back to 1913 shortly after the line's opening. Note the North British Railway notice on the extreme right. *Ian Allan Library (LGRP 7933)*

Now: 24 October 1998
The station is still open, but the station buildings have been altered and the immediate area has been redeveloped. *Author*

Glenfinnan

Then: 13 August 1960
The train, which consisted of six coaches and two vans, was too long for the platform at the station and, as a result, Motherwell-allocated Standard Class 4MT No 76001 has pulled up well clear of the platform. *Author*

Now: 24 October 1998
The station, which like the line opened on 1 April 1901, is still open and is busy, particularly during the summer season when it is much used by tourists. Little has changed over the past 38 years save for the disappearance of signalling and for the growth in the undergrowth. Note that the signalbox still stands in the background, although this is now redundant following the installation of RETB. *Author*

Lochailort

Then: 13 August 1960
Sporting a '66B' shedplate, Standard Class 4MT No 76001 of Motherwell pauses at Lochailort station with the 3.15pm service from Fort William to Mallaig. At this time, Lochailort was one of the many passing places on the mainly single track line from Fort William to Mallaig. *Author*

Now: 24 October 1998
Although the station is still open it sees few passengers and, as can be seen, the former loop provided in the up direction has disappeared. The station building has also disappeared, to be replaced by the much more utilitarian bus shelter-type structure visible on the platform. The magnificent scenery which forms a backdrop is, however, unchanged and unchanging. *Author*

Morar

Then: 1914
This view shows wagons in the siding at the west end of the station in the period shortly before the outbreak of World War 1. *Ian Allan Library (LGRP 8728)*

Arisaig

Then: Undated (c1913)
This station opened with the line on
1 April 1901.
Ian Allan Library (LGRP 7930)

Now: 24 October 1998
This station is remarkably unchanged
over the past 80 years. The signalbox
still stands (albeit disused since the
introduction of RETB) and both
platforms have retained their original
buildings. Arisaig is now one of the two
remaining passing places on the West
Highland Extension line to Mallaig.
Also still extant is the siding in the
background; this is, however, no longer
used for freight as the station lost its
freight facilities on 25 January 1965.
Author

Now: 24 October 1998
Considering that 84 years separate these
two photographs, very little has altered
at Morar except for the dramatic growth
in the trees and undergrowth. The
platform edgings are unchanged, if
examined closely, although there are
now no wagons and the siding has
disappeared. *Author*

Mallaig shed

Then: 22 July 1959
The little shed at Mallaig was only big enough to accommodate one locomotive. On this occasion, Eastfield-allocated Class K2 2-6-0 No 61764 *Loch Arkaig* was parked outside in light steam but with no booked work; my attempts to get it substituted for the booked 'K1' on the evening train to Fort William, however, failed. As a result, I was never able to have a trip behind a 'K2' on the West Highland. The turntable was to the left of the shed. *Author*

Now: 24 October 1998
The shed remained for many years after steam finished in the early 1960s; it always seemed to be full of fish crates from the local fishing industry. When the new road was built, the land around the shed was redeveloped into an industrial site and the old shed demolished. *Author*

Mallaig

Then: 13 August 1960
After working the 3.15pm service from Fort William, Motherwell-allocated Standard Class 4MT No 76001 carried out shunting duties at the east end of the station. This locomotive was on loan to Fort William for the summer 1960 timetable and put up an excellent performance on this day, gaining eight minutes from the late departure at Fort William. The station opened on 1 April 1901. The line on the left headed for the small shed and turntable. *Author*

Now: 24 October 1998
As this photograph shows, the trackwork here has been considerably rationalised over the past 38 years and to the left of the photograph is a new road. Class 37/4 No 37413 *The Scottish Railway Preservation Society*, together with sister locomotive No 37427, had just completed a complicated run-round manoeuvre of the 'Scottish Landcruise' train; this activity had involved splitting the train. The weather on this occasion, as so often with my visits to Mallaig, was terrible. *Author*

Portpatrick & Wigtownshire Joint Railway

Although the joint line only came into existence on 1 August 1885, the two railways which were to form the line were much older. As a joint company, the P&WJR was nominally controlled by the London & North Western, the Midland, the Caledonian and the Glasgow & South Western railways, although only the two Scottish-based railways actually operated over the route.

The first of the two constituents of the railway — the Portpatrick Railway — was authorised on 10 August 1857 to construct a railway from Castle Douglas — where an end-on junction was made with the G&SWR's Castle Douglas & Dumfries Railway (which was incorporated on 21 July 1856 and opened on 7 November 1859) — to Portpatrick with the intention of providing a link to Ireland via the shortest sea crossing between Great Britain and Ireland. The route opened through from Castle Douglas to Stranraer on 12 March 1861 and thence to Portpatrick on 28 August 1862. A harbour branch at Portpatrick opened on 1 October 1862. However, Portpatrick was soon overshadowed by the development of the port at Stranraer, which offered a safer and more sheltered environment.

The second constituent of the P&WJR was the Wigtownshire Railway. This was authorised to construct the line from Newton Stewart to Whithorn with a branch to Garlieston on 18 July 1872. The line opened from Newton Stewart to Wigtown on 3 April 1875 and thence to Millisle on 2 August 1875 and to the terminus at Whithorn on 9 July 1877. The ancillary branch to Garlieston opened on 3 August 1876. Passenger services on the latter ceased as early as 1 March 1903, but thereafter the line remained open for freight.

At the Grouping, given the fact that all four railways which owned the line passed into the hands of the LMS, the line ceased to have a joint status in 1923. All the lines inherited by the LMS passed into BR ownership in 1948, but the inexorable march of economic reality saw a gradual erosion of the ex-P&WJR routes. The branch to Whithorn and the line from Stranraer Town to Portpatrick lost their passenger services on 6 February 1950 and 25 September 1950 respectively. The section of line south from Golfin to Portpatrick closed completely in February 1950. The next casualty was the line from Stranraer south to Golfin, which closed completely on 1 April 1959. Next, the lines from Newton Stewart to Whithorn and Garlieston disappeared; freight services over the lines ceased on 5 October 1964. Finally, came the complete closure of the 'Port Road' itself, with services over the route ceasing on 14 June 1965. Stranraer Town station closed on 7 March 1966. Only two short sections — from Dumfries to Maxwelltown (for freight) and from Challoch Junction to Stranraer (freight and passenger) — survive (although the former is now disused).

Today, much of the line's infrastructure, including many of the dramatic viaducts, remains intact. Every now and again proposals appear to promote the line's reopening. However, the costs involved probably preclude this reconstruction.

Parton

Then: 11 June 1963
This bridge at Loch Ken was situated seven miles west of Castle Douglas and was at the end of the only really level section of track on the 'Port Road'. Here Stanier Class 5 No 44996 is at the head of a Stranraer-Carlisle train. The railway opened through Parton in March 1861. *Derek Cross*

New Galloway

Then: 31 August 1957
This station was situated almost nine miles west of Castle Douglas at the bottom of the four-mile climb at 1 in 80 to Loch Skerrow. The line opened on 12 March 1861. A Hughes 'Crab', No 42909, pauses on its way east at the head of a Stranraer-Dumfries freight. These locomotives worked the line for many years. *R. T. Hughes*

Now: 26 April 1998
Along with the rest of the 'Port Road' from Castle Douglas to Stranraer, the line through New Galloway closed completely on 14 June 1965. Today, most of the features — such as trackbed, station platform and road overbridge — are still extant, but the whole area has become very overgrown. *Author*

Now: 26 April 1998
The 'Port Road' through this location was to close completely on 14 June 1965. Little has altered over the years, except the track has been lifted and the trees have grown. Behind me, and alongside the loch, is a very pleasant caravan park. *Author*

Big Water of Fleet Viaduct

Then: 1 July 1961
This viaduct is situated about two miles east of Gatehouse of Fleet station, which is itself located in a very remote area and is at least six miles from the town it served. The station was, in fact, much closer to the small community of Dromore. The line opened in September 1861, at which time the station was called 'Dromore'; it only became 'Gatehouse' in 1863 and 'Gatehouse of Fleet' in 1912. The station was closed on 5 December 1949 but was surprisingly reopened on 20 May 1950. Here, a local Stanier Class 5, No 44885, is pictured heading for Stranraer; notice that my Triumph 21 motorcycle has also made an appearance in the photograph. *Author*

Now: 26 April 1998
The line through Gatehouse of Fleet closed completely on 14 June 1965 and the lines over the viaduct have long been lifted. Today it is possible to drive along the trackbed to the old station house, which has been converted into a dwelling, but otherwise there are few changes during the 37 years between the pictures. *Author*

Creetown

Then: 13 August 1964
Creetown, situated between Gatehouse of Fleet and Newton Stewart, is located about a mile from the village and was halfway up the 1 in 80 gradient from Palmure to Gatehouse of Fleet. This gradient was some six miles in length. The line at this point had opened on 12 March 1861. Stanier Class 5 No 45463 enters the station with a service to Dumfries. *Derek Cross*

Now: 26 April 1998
As the line had closed completely on 14 June 1965, I hardly expected to see any items of rolling stock here, and so I was surprised to see this brake van. The new owner of the property — and of the brake van — can be seen busy at work on the site; one day, the station will form a very nice — albeit remote — property. *Author*

Newton Stewart (west end)

Then: 27 May 1964
There is plenty to view in this very attractive picture, which was taken from the road bridge looking east. BR Standard Class 2MT No 78026 is caught shunting wagons from the Whithorn branch. The Portpatrick Railway from Castle Douglas to Stranraer opened on 12 March 1861; Newton Stewart became a junction on 3 April 1875 when the Wigtownshire Railway to Wigtown opened. *J. Spencer Gilks*

Now: 26 April 1998
The line through Newton Stewart closed completely on 14 June 1965, the branch to Whithorn having closed the previous October. Today the site of the station is occupied by the modern Royal Mail depot and by an industrial estate. There is little to remind readers that this was once a railway junction. *Author*

Wigtown

Then: 2 September 1961
A Stephenson Locomotive Society special from Glasgow visited the branches south of Newton Stewart in September 1961. The train was headed by ex-Caledonian Railway 'Jumbo' No 57375, which was shedded at Newton Stewart at that time. The line from Newton Stewart to Wigtown opened on 3 April 1875, being extended southwards four months later. Regular passenger services over the line ceased on 25 September 1950. Whilst, by the date of this photograph, it was some 11 years since the cessation of passenger services, the platform was still fit for use. *Author*

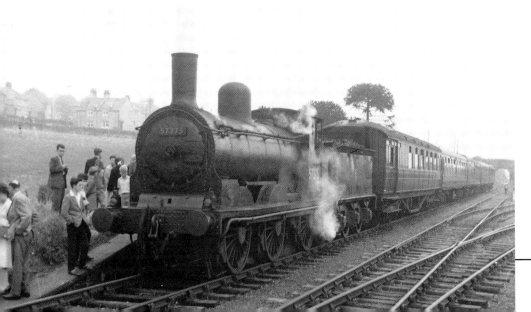

Newton Stewart shed

Then: 12 May 1957
This was the only shed located on the main line between Dumfries and Stranraer — a distance of over 73 miles. The shed's main function was to provide the locomotive for the Whithorn branch, which headed south from Newton Stewart. A couple of locomotives were present on shed when this visit by a group of enthusiasts who had travelled by coach from the Bradford area occurred. It was quite a day out in the days before motorways; the trip would have been at least 450 miles, all with one driver and all at the cost of around 25 shillings. *Author*

Now: 26 April 1998
The shed still stands and appears to be in use for storing caravans. I would have got a little closer in order to get a better viewpoint, but fortunately I spotted a very unfriendly Alsation dog just before it saw me! *Author*

Now: 26 April 1998
The line from Newton Stewart through Wigtown to Whithorn and Garlieston closed completely on 5 October 1964. The station area and trackbed have, since closure, passed into private hands, as can be seen from the more recent photograph. *Author*

Whauphill

Then: 26 April 1963
This station was situated about halfway along the Whithorn branch. The line from Newton Stewart to Wigtown opened on 3 April 1875; it was extended from Wigtown, through Whauphill, to Millisle on 2 August of the same year. This splendid branch line picture shows an Ivatt Class 2MT No 46467 leaving on a freight towards Whithorn. The train was probably due to shunt at the next station, Sorbie. Passenger services over the branch south from Newton Stewart ceased on 25 September 1950.
Derek Cross

Now: 26 April 1998
The freight services over the lines to Whithorn and Garlieston ceased on 5 October 1964. Today, the trackbed still exists as do the bridge and the platform edge (the latter in the undergrowth). Look, however, at how much the trees have grown over the past 35 years!
Author

Whithorn

Then: 27 May 1964
This was the terminus of the branch from Newton Stewart. The line from Millisle opened on 9 July 1877; the earlier (and shorter) branch from Millisle to Garlieston opened on 3 April 1876. The then thrice-weekly freight is being shunted in the yard by BR Standard No 78026. By this date passenger services had long ceased — being withdrawn on 25 September 1950 — and even freight was not destined for much longer. *J. Spencer Gilks*

Sorbie

Then: 2 September 1961
A further view of the Stephenson Locomotive Society railtour of September 1961 sees the special at Sorbie. The train called at most of the stations on the branch and, apart from the terrible weather, it was an excellent day out. Here it has stopped for passengers to inspect the station, which had lost its passenger services 11 years earlier. The section of line through Sorbie opened on 2 August 1875. *Author*

Now: 26 April 1998
It was quite difficult to sort out this location as the whole area had been developed and levelled since complete closure on 5 October 1964. Fortunately, the station house on the left-hand side still existed as a private dwelling. The Galloway Granite Co now owns the site. *Author*

Now: 26 April 1998
Some five months after the 'Then' photograph, on 5 October 1964, freight services over the line from Newton Stewart to Whithorn and Garlieston were finally withdrawn. The changes here over the past 34 years have been dramatic. I was told that the factory in the 'Then' photograph became disused and was later destroyed by fire, allegedly the result of vandalism. The whole site was cleared and is now, ironically, occupied by the local fire service. Part of the site is also occupied by Stagecoach, but there were no buses when I visited. *Author*

Glenluce

Then: 2 September 1961
Following its trip along the Whithorn branch, the Stephenson
Locomotive Society special headed west towards Stranraer. Here the
train's locomotive, ex-CR No 57375 is pictured taking water at
Glenluce, which was the final station before the junction with the
G&SWR line on the approaches to Stranraer. The station was
situated 64 miles west of Dumfries and opened on 12 March 1861.
Author

Now: 26 April 1998
Since the line's complete closure on 14 June 1965, new houses have
been built on the site. Everything associated with the railway has
vanished with the exception of the road bridge, which can just be
seen in the background. *Author*

Stranraer Harbour

Then: 11 June 1965
The station opened on 1 October 1862. These InterCity Swindon-built DMUs became Class 126s under the TOPS scheme; this unit has just arrived on the 11.25 from Glasgow and is pictured leaving the station as empty stock. *Colin T. Gifford*

Now: 26 April 1998
When the 'Port Road' was operational it was just over 73 miles to Dumfries; today, the journey can still be made, but it is now 135 miles via Kilmarnock. The layout at Stranraer Harbour has not changed much over the years, but the ship and cars certainly have. The port and Cairnryan across Loch Ryan are still very busy, but mainly with 'Seacats'. Locomotive-hauled trains are very infrequent, with the passenger services now entirely in the hands of Class 156 Sprinters. Here unit No 156467 is ready to leave on the 19.41 to Glasgow. *Author*

List of Locations

Stranraer Town

Then: 12 July 1963
The station opened here on 12 March 1861 and the line once continued through to Portpatrick, until the section of line beyond Stranraer was closed to passengers on 6 February 1950 and between Stranraer and Golfin for freight on 16 April 1959 (the section between Golfin and Portpatrick closed completely in February 1950). This station was originally known as simply 'Stranraer', becoming 'Stranraer Town' on 2 March 1953. Stanier Class 5 No 45432 has just come off the stock of the 8.57am service from Castle Douglas in the station. *Michael Mensing*

Now: 26 April 1998
Although the station lost its passenger services on 7 March 1966, it still stands and the yards to the right are still intact, but virtually unused at the present time. It is hoped, however, that EWS may gain some traffic in the near future from this location. Above the station stands the old steam shed, which appears to be used by a scrap metal merchant. *Author*